The Art of Meditation

The Art of Meditation

MATTHIEU RICARD

Translated by
Sherab Chödzin Kohn

Atlantic Books
LONDON

First published in France as *L'art de la meditation* in 2008 by NiL éditions, Paris.

First published in English in Great Britain in 2010 by Atlantic Books,
an imprint of Grove Atlantic Ltd.

2 3 4 5 6 7 8 9

A CIP catalogue record for this book is available
from the British Library.

ISBN: 978 1 84887 075 8

Printed in Great Britain by Clays Ltd, St Ives plc

Atlantic Books
An imprint of Grove Atlantic Ltd
Ormond House
26–27 Boswell Street
London
WC1N 3JZ

www.atlantic-books.co.uk

The Art of Meditation

Contents

Foreword

We must *be* the change we want to see in the world.

— Gandhi

WHY THIS LITTLE BOOK ON MEDITATION? FOR FORTY years I have had the good fortune to study with authentic spiritual masters who inspired me and illuminated my path in life. Their precious instructions have guided my actions. I am not a teacher — I remain more than ever a student — but in the course of my travels round the world, I have frequently met people who have shared with me their wish to learn to meditate. I have tried to the best of my ability to direct them to qualified teachers, but this has not always been possible. So it is for all those people who have a sincere desire to meditate that I have collected these instructions, drawn from authentic Buddhist sources, into book form.

The real significance of meditation is inner transformation through training the mind, which is a really exciting adventure. The exercises you will find here are taken from a tradition that is more than two thousand years old. It is best to explore them gradually, but you may also practise them independently of each other, whether you devote only thirty minutes a day to meditation or practise it more intensively in the undisturbed environment of a retreat.

As to my personal history, I had the tremendous good fortune of meeting my spiritual master, Kangyur Rinpoche, in 1967 near Darjeeling in India. I owe him whatever goodness there is in my life. After his death in 1975, I spent several years in retreat in a small wooden hut built on stilts in the forest above his monastery. For a period of thirteen years, starting in 1981, I had the privilege of living in the presence of the great master Dilgo Khyentse Rinpoche and receiving his teachings. Since 1991 when he departed this world, I have often stayed in retreat in a small mountain hermitage in Nepal, a few hours away from Kathmandu, in a contemplative centre founded by the Shechen Monastery, where I usually reside. These periods of retreat have without a doubt been among the most fertile times of my life.

Over the course of the last ten years, I have also participated in several scientific research programmes intended to document the long-term effects of meditation practice on the brain and on behaviour. This research has shown that it is possible to make significant progress in developing qualities such as attention, emotional balance, altruism and inner peace. Other studies have also demonstrated the benefits of meditating for twenty minutes a day for a period of six to eight weeks. These benefits include a decrease in anxiety, in vulnerability to pain and in the tendency towards depression and anger, as well as strengthening attention, the immune system and an increase in general well-being. Thus no matter what point of view you approach it from – from that of personal transformation, the development of altruistic love or physical health – meditation emerges as a factor essential for leading a balanced life, rich in meaning.

It is a pity to underestimate the capacity we have to

transform our mind. Each of us possesses the potential needed to free ourselves from the mental states that perpetuate our own suffering and that of others — the potential to find our own inner peace and contribute to the welfare of others.

PART I

Why Meditate?

Take a sincere look at yourself. Where are you in your life? What have your priorities been up till now and what do you intend doing with the time you have left?

We are a mixture of light and shadow, of good qualities and faults. Are we really the best we can be? Must we remain as we are now? If not, what can we do to improve ourselves? These are questions worth asking, particularly if we have come to the conclusion that change is both desirable and possible.

In the West, we are consumed from morning till night by endless activity. We do not have much time or energy left over to consider the basic causes of our happiness or suffering. We imagine, more or less consciously, that if we undertake more activities we will have more intense experiences and, therefore, our sense of dissatisfaction will fade away. But the truth is that many of us continue to feel let down and frustrated by our contemporary lifestyle.

The aim of meditation is to transform the mind. It does not have to be associated with any particular religion. Every one of us has a mind and every one of us can work on it.

Is Change Desirable?

There are very few people who would say that there is nothing worth improving in the way they live and experience the world. However, some people think their own particular weaknesses and conflicting emotions are something rich that contributes to the fullness of their lives. They believe this particular alchemy in their character is what makes them unique and think they should learn to accept themselves the way they are. They do not realize that this kind of thinking can lead to a life of chronic discontent. Nor do they realize that they could help themselves with just a little reflection and effort.

Imagine someone suggested you spend an entire day tormented by jealousy. Would you want to do that? I doubt it. If, on the other hand, someone suggested you spend that same day with your heart filled with love for all beings, you would probably be quite willing to do so. I'm sure you would find that infinitely preferable to a whole day of jealousy.

As things stand now, no matter what our preferences might be, our mind is often filled with troubles. We spend a great deal of time consumed by painful thoughts, plagued by anxiety or anger, licking the wounds we receive from other people's harsh words. When we experience these kinds of difficult moments, we wish we could manage our emotions; we wish we could master our mind to the point where we could be free of these afflicting emotions. It would be such a relief. However, since we don't know how to achieve this kind of control, we take the point of view that, after all, this way of living is 'normal' or 'natural', and that it is 'human nature'. Even if it were natural, that would not make it desirable. Illness, for example, comes to everybody, but does this prevent us from consulting a doctor?

We don't want to suffer. Nobody wakes up in the morning and thinks: 'Oh, if I could only suffer all day today and, if possible, every day for the rest of my life!' Whatever we are occupied with – an important task, routine work, walking in the woods, pursuing a relationship, drinking a cup of tea – we always hope we will get some benefit or satisfaction out of it, either for ourselves or others. If we thought nothing would come of our activities but suffering, we wouldn't do anything at all and we would fall into despair.

Sometimes we do have moments of inner peace, of altruistic love, of deep-felt confidence, but, for the most part, these are only fleeting experiences that quickly give way to other less pleasant ones. What if we could train our mind to cultivate these wholesome moments? No doubt it would radically change our lives for the better. Wouldn't it be wonderful to become better human beings and lead lives in which we experience inner fulfilment, while also relieving the suffering of others and contributing to their well-being?

Some people think life would be dull without inner conflict but we are all familiar with the suffering that accompanies anger, greed or jealousy, and we all appreciate the good feelings that go along with kindness, contentment and the pleasure of seeing other people happy. The sense of harmony that is connected with loving others has an inherent goodness in it that speaks for itself. The same is true of generosity, patience, emotional balance and many other positive traits. If we could learn to cultivate altruistic love and inner calm, and if at the same time the self-centred approach of the ego and the frustration that arises from it could be reduced, then our lives certainly would not lose any of their richness – quite the opposite.

Is Change Possible?

So the real question is not whether change is desirable; it is whether it is possible to change. Some people might think they can't change because their afflictive emotions are so intimately associated with their minds that it is impossible to get rid of them without destroying a part of themselves.

It is true that in general people's characters don't change very much. If we could study the same group of people every few years, we would rarely find that the angry people had become patient, that the disturbed people had found inner peace, or that the pretentious people had learned humility. But as rare as such changes might be some people *do* change, which shows that change *is* possible. The point is that our negative character traits tend to persist if we don't do anything to change the status quo. No change occurs if we just let our habitual tendencies and automatic patterns of thought perpetuate and even reinforce themselves thought after thought, day after day, year after year. But those tendencies and patterns can be challenged.

Aggression, greed, jealousy and the other mental poisons are unquestionably part of us, but are they an inalienable part? Not necessarily. For example, a glass of water might contain cyanide that could kill us on the spot. But the same water could also be mixed with healing medicine. In either case, H_2O, the chemical formula of the water itself, remains unchanged; in itself, it was never either poisonous or medicinal. The different states of the water are temporary and circumstantial. Our emotions, moods and bad character traits are just temporary and circumstantial elements of our nature.

A Fundamental Aspect of Consciousness

This temporary and circumstantial quality becomes clear to us when we realize that the primary quality of consciousness, which is comparable to the water in the example above, is simply knowing. Knowing in itself is neither good nor bad. If we look behind the turbulent stream of transient thoughts and emotions that pass through our mind day and night, this fundamental aspect of consciousness, knowing, which makes possible and underlies all perception no matter what its nature, is always there. Buddhism describes this knowing aspect of the mind as luminous, because it illuminates both the external world and the inner world of sensation, emotion, reasoning, memory, hope and fear.

Although this faculty of knowing underlies every mental event, it is not itself *affected* by any of these events. A ray of light may shine on a face disfigured by hatred or on a smiling face, it may shine on a jewel or on a garbage heap; but the light itself is neither mean nor loving, neither dirty nor clean. Understanding that the essential nature of consciousness is neutral permits us to understand that it is possible to change our mental universe. We can transform the content of our thoughts and experiences. The neutral and luminous background of our consciousness provides us with the space we need to observe mental events, rather than being at their mercy, and then to create the conditions necessary to transform them.

Just Wishing is Not Enough

We have no choice about what we already are, but we can wish to change ourselves. Such an aspiration can give the mind a sense of direction. But just wishing is not enough. We have to find a way of putting that wish into action.

We don't find anything strange about spending years learning to walk, to read and write or to acquire professional skills. We spend hours doing physical exercises in order to get our bodies fit. Sometimes we expend tremendous physical energy pedalling a stationary bike that goes nowhere. To sustain such tasks, we have to have a minimum of interest or enthusiasm. This interest comes from feeling that, in the long run, these efforts are going to benefit us.

Working with the mind follows the same logic. How could it be subject to change without the least effort, just from wishing alone? That doesn't make any more sense than expecting to learn to play a Mozart sonata just by occasionally doodling around on the piano.

We expend a lot of effort to improve the external conditions of our lives, but in the end it is always the mind that creates our experience of the world and translates it into well-being or suffering. If we transform our way of perceiving things, we transform the quality of our lives. It is this kind of transformation that is brought about by the form of mind-training known as meditation.

What is Meditation?

Meditation is a practice that makes it possible to cultivate and develop certain basic positive human qualities in the same way as other forms of training make it possible to play a musical instrument or acquire any other skill.

The words that are translated into English as meditation are *bhavana* from Sanskrit, which means 'to cultivate', and *gom* from the Tibetan, which means 'to become familiar with'. Primarily, meditation is a matter of familiarizing ourselves with a clear and accurate way of seeing things and of cultivating the good qualities that remain dormant inside us until we make the effort to bring them out.

So let us begin by asking ourselves, 'What do I really want out of life? Am I content to just keep improvising from day to day? Am I going to overlook the vague sense of discontent that I always feel deep down when, at the same time, I am longing for well-being and fulfilment?'

We have become accustomed to thinking that our faults are inevitable and that we have to put up with the setbacks they have brought us throughout our lives. We have come to take the dysfunctional aspect of ourselves for granted without realizing that it is possible to free ourselves from the vicious circle that is exhausting us.

From a Buddhist point of view, every being has the potential for enlightenment just as surely, say the traditional texts, as every sesame seed contains oil. Despite this, to use another traditional comparison, we wander about in confusion like a beggar who is simultaneously both rich and poor because he does not know that he has a treasure buried under the floor of his hut. The goal of the Buddhist path is to come into possession of this overlooked wealth of ours, which can imbue our lives with the most profound meaning.

Transforming Ourselves to Better Transform the World

Developing our own positive inner qualities is the best way to help others. At the beginning, our personal experience is our only reference point but, as we continue, it can become the basis for a much larger point of view that includes all beings. We are all dependent on each other, and none of us wants to suffer. Being happy in the midst of an infinite number of other beings who are suffering is absurd (if it were even possible). Seeking happiness for oneself alone is doomed to certain failure, since self-centredness is the very source of our discontent. 'When selfish happiness is the only goal in life, life soon becomes goalless,' wrote the French novelist Romain Rolland.[1]

Even if we show all the outward signs of happiness, we cannot be truly happy if we fail to take an interest in the happiness of others. Altruistic love and compassion are the foundations of genuine happiness.

These remarks are not intended to be moralistic; they simply reflect reality. Seeking happiness selfishly is the best way there is to make yourself, or anyone else, unhappy. Some people might think that the smartest way to guarantee their own well-being is to isolate themselves from others and to work hard at their own happiness, without consideration for other people. They probably assume that if everybody does that, we'll all be happy. But the result would be exactly the opposite: instead of being happy, they would be torn between hope and fear, make their own lives miserable and ruin the lives of the people around them as well. In the end, just 'looking out for number one' is a losing proposition for everybody. One of the fundamental reasons such an approach is doomed is that the world is not made up of independent entities endowed with intrinsic properties that make them by nature beautiful or ugly, friends or enemies. Things and beings are essentially interdependent and in a constant state of transformation. The very elements that compose them only exist in relationship to each other. The self-centred approach of the ego continually runs afoul of this reality and only succeeds in creating frustration.

Altruistic love, according to Buddhism, is the wish that others be happy, an attitude that consists of wishing others to be happy and find the true causes of happiness. Compassion is defined as the desire to put an end to the suffering of others and the causes of that suffering. These are not merely noble sentiments; they are feelings that are fundamentally in tune with reality. All beings want to avoid suffering just as much as we do. Moreover, since we are all interdependent, our own happiness and un-happiness are intimately bound up with the happiness and unhappiness of others. Cultivating love and compassion is a win–win situation. Personal experience shows that they are the most positive of all mental states and create a deep sense of fulfilment and wholesomeness. Research in neuroscience also indicates that among all kinds of meditations those focusing on unconditional love and compassion give rise to the strongest activation of brain areas related to positive affects. In addition, the behaviour they give rise to is intended to benefit others.

In order for the deeds we perform for the sake of others to have the intended benefit, they must also be guided by wisdom – the wisdom that we can acquire through meditation. The ultimate reason for meditating is to transform ourselves in order to be better able to transform the world or, to put it another way, to transform ourselves so we can become better human beings in order to serve others in a wiser and more efficient way. It gives your life the noblest possible meaning.

A Universal Effect

The primary goal of meditation is to transform our experience of the world, but it has also been shown that meditation has beneficial effects on our health. For the last ten years, inspired by the catalytic activities of the Mind and Life Institute, dedicated to the collaboration between Buddhism and modern science, major American universities such as the University of Wisconsin in Madison, Princeton, Harvard and the University of California at Berkeley, as well as research centres in Zurich,

Switzerland, have been conducting intensive studies on meditation and its long- and short-term effects on the brain. Experienced meditators who have meditated for between ten and sixty thousand hours have demonstrated qualities of focused attention that are not found among beginners. For example, they are able to maintain more or less perfect concentration on a particular task for forty-five minutes, whereas most people cannot go beyond five or ten minutes before they begin making an increasing number of mistakes.

Experienced meditators are able to generate precise targeted mental states that are enduring and powerful. Among other things, experiments have shown that the region of the brain associated with mental states like compassion exhibits considerably greater activity among persons who have long meditative experience than among those who have not. These discoveries demonstrate that certain human qualities can be deliberately cultivated through mental training. Such studies have led to the publication of several articles in prestigious scientific journals, establishing the credibility of research on meditation, an area which had not been taken seriously until then. In the words of Richard Davidson, a leading neuroscientist, 'These studies seem to demonstrate that the brain can be trained and physically modified in a way that few people would have imagined.'[2]

Other scientific investigations have also shown that you do not have to be a highly trained meditator to benefit from the effects of meditation, and that twenty minutes of daily practice can contribute significantly to the reduction of stress, whose harmful effects on health are well established.[3] It also reduces anxiety, the tendency towards anger (which diminishes the chances of survival following heart surgery), and the risk of relapse for people who have previously undergone at least two episodes of serious depression.[4] Eight weeks of meditation (of the type known as MBSR[5]) for thirty minutes a day significantly strengthens the immune system, reinforces positive emotions[6] and the faculty of attention,[7] and reduces arterial pressure in those suffering from high blood pressure,[8] as well as accelerating the healing of psoriasis.[9]

To what extent can we train our mind to work in a constructive manner — to replace obsession with contentment, agitation with calmness, hatred with kindness?

Twenty years ago, it was almost universally accepted by neuroscientists that the brain contained all its neurons at birth, and that their number did not change in adult life. We now know that new neurons are produced up until the moment of death, and we speak of 'neuroplasticity', a term which takes into account the fact that the brain evolves continuously in relation to our experience, and that a particular training, such as learning a musical instrument or a sport, can bring about a profound change. Mindfulness, altruism and other basic human qualities can be cultivated in the same way. In general, if we engage repeatedly in a new activity or train in a new skill, modifications in the neuronal system of the brain can be observed within a month. What is essential, therefore, is to meditate regularly.

Study of the influence of our mental states on our way of being and our health, which was once considered a purely eccentric notion, is now becoming a mainstream approach in scientific research.[10] The increasingly powerful Magnetic Resonance Imaging (MRI) techniques and sophisticated electroencephalograms (EEG) as well as magneto encephalography (MEG), combined with the participation of experienced contemplatives, have led us towards a golden age of contemplative neuroscience. It is a fascinating prospect, and there is so much more to discover.

A full life is not made up of an uninterrupted succession of pleasant sensations but really comes from transforming the way we understand and work through the challenges of our existence. Training the mind not only makes it possible to cope with mental toxins like hatred, obsession and fear that poison our existence, but also helps us acquire a better understanding of how the mind functions and gives us a more accurate perception of reality. This, in turn, gives us the inner resources to successfully face the highs and lows of life without being distracted or broken by them, and allows us to draw deep lessons from them.

One of the great tragedies of our time is that we significantly underestimate our capacity for change. Our character traits remain the same as long as we do nothing to change them, and as long as we continue to tolerate and reinforce our habits and patterns, thought after thought.

The truth is that the state we generally consider to be

'normal' is just a starting point and not the goal we ought to set for ourselves. Our life is worth much more than that! It is possible, little by little, to arrive at an 'optimal' way of being.

I cannot emphasize enough how much meditation and mind training can change our lives and bring about an inner revolution, which is profound and peaceful and affects the quality of every moment of our experience.

Source of Inspiration

Unfortunately, one of the main obstacles we face when we try to examine the mind is a deep-seated and often unconscious conviction that 'we're born the way we are and nothing we can do can change that'. I experienced this same sense of pessimistic futility during my own childhood, and I've seen it reflected again and again in my work with people around the world. Without even consciously thinking about it, the idea that we can't alter our minds blocks our every attempt to try.

People I've spoken with who try to make a change using aspirations, prayers, or visualizations admit that they often give up after a few days or weeks because they don't see any immediate results. When their prayers and aspirations don't work, they dismiss the whole idea of working with the mind as a marketing gimmick designed to sell books... [However] during my conversations with scientists around the world, I've been amazed to see that there is a nearly universal consensus in the scientific community that the brain is structured in a way that actually does make it possible to effect real changes in everyday experience.

—*Yongey Mingyur Rinpoche*[11]

PART II

What to Meditate On?

THE OBJECT OF MEDITATION IS THE MIND. FOR THE moment, it is simultaneously confused, agitated, rebellious and subject to innumerable conditioned and automatic patterns. The goal of meditation is not to shut down the mind or anaesthetise it, but rather to make it free, lucid and balanced.

According to Buddhism, the mind is not an entity but rather a dynamic stream of experiences, a succession of moments of consciousness. These experiences are often marked by confusion and suffering, but we can also live them in a spacious state of clarity and inner freedom.

We all well know, as the contemporary Tibetan master Jigme Khyentse Rinpoche reminds us, that 'we don't need to train our minds to improve our ability to get upset or jealous. We don't need an anger accelerator or a pride amplifier.'[12] By contrast, training the mind is crucial if we want to refine and sharpen our attention, develop emotional balance, inner peace and wisdom, and cultivate dedication to the welfare of others. We have within ourselves the potential to develop these qualities, but they will not develop by themselves or just because we want them to. They require training. And all training requires perseverance and enthusiasm, as I have already said. We won't learn to ski by practising one or two minutes a month.

Refining Attention and Mindfulness

Galileo discovered the rings of Saturn after devising a telescope that was sufficiently bright and powerful and setting it up on a stable support. His discovery would not have been possible if his instrument had been inadequate or if he had held it in a trembling hand. Similarly, if we want to observe the subtlest mechanisms of our mental functioning and have an effect on them, we absolutely must refine our powers of looking inward. In order to do that our attention has to be highly sharpened so that it becomes stable and clear. We will then be able to observe how the mind functions and perceives the world and we will be able to understand the way thoughts multiply by association. Finally, we will be able to continue to refine the mind's perception until we reach the point where we are able to see the most fundamental state of our consciousness, a perfectly lucid and awakened state that is always present, even in the absence of discursive thoughts.

What Meditation is Not

Sometimes practitioners of meditation are accused of being too focused on themselves, of wallowing in egocentric introspection and failing to be concerned with others. But we cannot regard as selfish a process whose goal is to root out the obsession with self and to cultivate altruism. This would be like blaming an aspiring doctor for spending years studying medicine before beginning to practise.

There are a fair number of clichés in circulation concerning meditation. I should point out right away that meditation is not trying to create a void in one's mind by blocking out thoughts — which is impossible anyway. Nor is it engaging the mind in endless cogitation in an attempt to analyse the past or anticipate the future. Neither is it a simple process of relaxation in which inner conflicts are temporarily suspended in a vague amorphous state of consciousness. There is not much point in resting in a state of inner bewilderment.

There is indeed an element of relaxation in meditation, but it is connected with the relief that comes from letting go of hopes and fears, of attachments and the whims of the ego that never stop feeding our inner conflicts.

A Mastery That Sets Us Free

As we shall see, the way we deal with thoughts in meditation is not to block or feed them indefinitely, but to let them rise and dissolve by themselves in the field of mindfulness. In this way, they do not take over our minds.

Beyond that, meditation consists in cultivating a way of being that is not subject to the patterns of habitual thinking. It often begins with analysis and then continues with contemplation and inner transformation.

To be free is to be the master of ourselves. It is not a matter of doing whatever comes into our heads, but rather of freeing ourselves from the constraints and afflictions that dominate and obscure our minds. It is a matter of taking our life into our own hands rather than abandoning it to the tendencies created by habit and mental confusion. Instead of letting go of the helm and just letting the boat drift wherever the wind blows, freedom means setting a course towards a chosen destination – the destination that we know to be the most desirable for ourselves and others.

At the Heart of Reality

Meditation is not a means of escaping reality, as some people think. On the contrary, its object is to make us see reality as it is right in the midst of our experience, to unmask the deep causes of our suffering and to dispel mental confusion. We develop a kind of understanding that comes from a clearer view of reality. To reach this understanding, we meditate, for example, on the interdependence of all phenomena, on their transitory character and on the non-existence of the ego perceived as a solid and independent entity.

Meditations on these themes are based on the experience of generations of meditators who have devoted their lives to observing the automatic, mechanical patterns of thought and the nature of consciousness. They then taught empirical methods for developing mental clarity, alertness, inner freedom, altruistic love and compassion. However, we cannot merely rely on their words to free ourselves from suffering. We must discover for ourselves the value of the methods these wise people taught and confirm for ourselves the conclusions they reached. This is not purely an intellectual process. Long study of our own experience is needed in order to rediscover their answers and integrate them into ourselves on a deep level. This process requires determination, enthusiasm and perseverance. It requires what Shantideva calls, 'the joy of doing what is beneficial'.[13]

Thus we begin by observing and understanding how thoughts multiply by association with each other and create a whole world of emotions, of joy and suffering. Then we penetrate behind the screen of thoughts and glimpse the fundamental component of consciousness, the primal cognitive faculty out of which all thoughts arise.

Liberating the Monkey Mind

To accomplish this task, we must begin by calming our turbulent mind. Our mind behaves like a captive monkey who, in his agitation, becomes more and more entangled in his bonds.

Out of the vortex of our thoughts, firstly emotions arise and then moods and behaviours, then, finally, habits and traits of character. What arises spontaneously does not necessarily produce good results, any more than throwing seeds into the wind produces good harvests. So we have to behave as a good farmer does who prepares his field before sowing his seeds. For us, this means that the most important task is to attain freedom through mastering our mind.

If we consider that the possible benefit of meditation is to have a new experience of the world each moment of our lives, then it doesn't seem excessive to spend at least twenty minutes a day getting to know our mind better and training it towards this kind of openness. The fruition of meditation could be described as an optimal way of being, or again, as genuine happiness. This true and lasting happiness is a profound sense of having realized to the utmost the potential we have within us for wisdom and accomplishment. Working towards this kind of fulfilment is an adventure worth embarking on.

PART III

How to Meditate?

MEDITATION IS NOT A MATTER OF THEORY BUT OF practice, just as it does not satisfy your hunger to read a restaurant menu if you are not going to eat something from it. Nevertheless, it is an invaluable help to be able to consult the guidelines for meditation found in the works of the sages of the past. These works are treasure mines of instruction, which clearly expound the goal and methods of meditation, describe the best way to practise it and deal with the pitfalls that may await the practitioner.

Let us look now at some of these teachings. Let's begin with preliminary instructions and general advice, and then move on to some of the numerous methods of meditation. The descriptions will be kept simple so that these practices can be approached easily and gradually. Those who want to go into them more deeply will find references to more detailed works in the bibliography at the end of the book. The importance of an experienced living guide can never be overemphasized. It is not the intention of this book to replace such a guide. The aim is solely to provide some basic instruction derived from authentic sources.

A number of the exercises that follow, especially those dealing with mindfulness, inner calm, deep insight and altruistic love, are common to all schools of Buddhism. Others, for example those dealing with the emotions, come from the teachings of Tibetan Buddhism. Since this book is aimed particularly at readers who want to practise meditation without necessarily becoming Buddhists, certain essentials of Buddhist practice such as taking refuge and other specifically Buddhist topics will not be explained here. These can be found in many insightful texts, such as *The Words of My Perfect Teacher* by Patrul Rinpoche or the commentary of *The Treasury of Precious*

Qualities by Kangyur Rinpoche (Longchen Yeshe Dorje). In essence, let us remember that our mind can be our best friend or our worst enemy. Thus liberating it from confusion, the self-centredness of the ego and afflictive emotions is the greatest favour we can do ourselves and others.

Motivation

As with any other action, when we begin to practise a particular meditation, it is essential to be sure about our motivation. For it is our motivation, altruistic or self-centred, vast or limited, that will give the journey we are about to take a positive or negative direction and thus determine its results.

We would all like to avoid suffering and attain happiness, and we all have the basic right to fulfil these wishes. However, our deeds are in conflict with our aspirations most of the time. We look for happiness where it doesn't exist and we rush headlong towards what makes us suffer. Buddhist practice does not ask us to give up what is really good in life, but rather to abandon the causes of suffering, to which we are often addicted as to drugs. Suffering is caused by mental confusion that dims our clarity and judgement. The only way to remedy this is to develop an accurate view of reality and transform our minds. This is what will enable us to eliminate the primary causes of suffering: the mental poisons of ignorance, aggression, greed, pride and jealousy, which in turn are caused by our self-centred and delusional attachment to the ego.

Buddhism refers to several kinds of suffering. Visible suffering is evident everywhere. Hidden suffering is related to impermanence and change, and can conceal itself beneath the appearance of pleasure. An even deeper and less visible aspect of suffering comes from our basic ignorance and will stay with us as long as we remain in the grip of delusion and selfishness.

Over 2,500 years ago, after attaining enlightenment under the Bodhi tree, the Buddha gave his first teaching in the Deer Park outside Varanasi. There he taught the Four Noble Truths. The first is the truth of suffering, which needs to be recognized. The second is the truth of the causes of suffering – ignorance that engenders craving, hatred, pride, jealousy and many other thoughts that poison our lives and those of others. Since these mental poisons can be eliminated, an end to suffering – the third truth – is therefore possible. The fourth truth is the path that turns that potential into reality. The path is the process of using all available means to eliminate the fundamental causes of suffering.

But just getting rid of our own suffering is not enough. Each of us is just one person, while the number of other beings is infinite. All those other beings want to avoid suffering as much as we do. Moreover, all beings are interdependent, so we are intimately connected with all those others. So the ultimate goal of meditation is to acquire the ability to liberate all beings from suffering and contribute to their well-being.

Sections entitled 'Meditation' contain concise and practical descriptions of various kinds of meditations. After carefully reading these instructions, try to bring them into your experience during the meditation session, so that they become part of your mind-stream.

'Sources of Inspiration' offer teachings and instructions spoken or written by great masters, which clarify, enrich, and deepen the various meditations proposed in the exercises.

Meditation

Reflect on how you are now. Do you find patterns of behaviour and habitual reactions in yourself that need to be improved or transformed? Look into the deepest part of yourself. Can you sense the presence of a potential for change there? Arouse the confidence to believe that change is possible through effort, determination and wisdom. Take a vow to transform yourself not only for your own sake, but also, and especially, for the sake of one day being able to dispel the suffering of others and contribute to their enduring happiness. Let this determination grow and take root in the deepest part of your being.

Sources of Inspiration

Do our actions demonstrate narrowness or openness of mind? Do we take a whole situation into consideration or do we limit ourselves to the details? Do we have a short- or long-term perspective? Is our compassion confined to our family, our friends and the people we identify with? We must continually reflect on these points.

—*14th Dalai Lama*[14]

May the precious Thought of Enlightenment
Be born in me if I have not already given birth to it.
Having been born, may it never wane
But always become greater.

—*The Bodhisattva Vow*[15]

Conditions Conducive to the Practice of Meditation

FOLLOWING THE ADVICE OF A QUALIFIED GUIDE

To start meditating you have to know how to go about it, which is why a competent instructor is essential. In the best of cases this will be an authentic spiritual master who represents an inexhaustible source of wisdom and inspiration as well as long personal experience. In truth, nothing can replace the exemplary power and profundity of transmission from a living master. In addition to the master's inspiring presence and the teaching that he transmits constantly just by his way of being, he also makes sure that the student does not get sidetracked.

If you do not have the opportunity to meet such a master, you can also benefit from the advice of a person who has more knowledge and experience than you do and whose instructions are based on a proven contemplative tradition. If that too is not possible, the best thing is to get help from a text, even a very simple one like the present book, which is drawn from trustworthy sources. That is preferable to putting yourself in the hands of someone whose teachings are little more than home-made concoctions.

A SUITABLE PLACE FOR MEDITATION

Our time and our minds tend to be taken up by all kinds of activities and preoccupations that never seem to end. That is why, in the beginning stage, we need to set up certain favourable conditions. Of course, the good effects of meditation can last and continue into our everyday life, especially through the practice of mindfulness, but to begin with, we need to train our mind in a protected environment.

You don't learn the basics of navigation in the thick of a storm; you learn them in good weather on a calm sea. In the same way, it is best in the beginning to meditate in a quiet place where there is space for the mind to develop clarity and stability. A comparison frequently given in the Buddhist texts is the flame of an oil lamp. If it is continually exposed to the wind, its light will be weak and in constant danger of being blown out. On the other hand, if the flame is protected from the wind by a glass cover, it will be stable and bright. The same sort of consideration applies to our minds.

AN APPROPRIATE PHYSICAL POSTURE

Your physical posture affects your mental state. If you take a posture that is too relaxed, especially if you lie down, the chances are that your meditation will stray into drowsiness. Too rigid and tense a posture, on the other hand, might well lead to mental agitation. Thus it is appropriate to take a balanced posture that is neither too tight nor too loose. In the texts, there is a description with seven points, called the posture of Vairochana.

1. The legs are crossed in the *vajra* posture, often called the lotus position. You begin by folding the right leg over the left, then the left over the right. If this is too difficult, you can use the half-lotus posture, also known as the tailor's position, in which one foot is brought on top of the opposite thigh and the other foot rests under the other thigh.

2. The hands rest, palms up, on the lap in the

posture of equanimity, with the right hand on top of the left and the tips of the thumbs touching each other. A second variation is letting the hands rest flat, palms down, on the knees

3. The shoulders are slightly raised and turned slightly forward.

4. The spinal column is quite straight 'like a pile of gold coins'.

5. The chin is tucked in slightly towards the throat.

6. The tip of the tongue touches the palate, near the front teeth.

7. The gaze is directed straight ahead or slightly down, following the line of the nose. The eyes are wide open or half closed.

If you have difficulty staying in a cross-legged position, then it is fine to meditate in a chair or on a raised cushion. The essential is to maintain a balanced posture with the back straight and follow the other posture points described above. It is said in the traditional texts that if the body is quite straight, the subtle energy channels will also be straight and, as a result, the mind will be clear.

Nevertheless, it is all right to modify your position slightly in accordance with the way your meditation is going. If you have a tendency to sink into apathy or even sleep, you can straighten your torso and adopt a more energetic posture while directing your gaze upwards. If, on the contrary, your mind is too agitated, you can relax your posture a bit and gaze downward.

You should maintain a suitable posture for as long as you can, but if it becomes too uncomfortable, it is better to relax for a few moments than be constantly distracted by pain. You can also, to the extent you are able, turn your attention directly to the experience of pain without either rejecting or amplifying it. Merely take it in as you would any other sensation, pleasant or unpleasant, as part of your mindfulness of the present moment. Also, you can alternate periods of sitting meditation with periods of walking meditation, a method that will be described later on.

Enthusiasm as the Driving Force Behind Perseverance

In order to arouse enough interest in something to devote some time to it, you have to see its advantages. Contemplating the benefits that can be expected from meditation and then tasting them a little bit will nourish your interest. However, this does not mean to say that the practice of meditation is always pleasant. An expedition into the mountains is not always purely fun. In addition to wonderful moments in breathtaking landscapes, we can also face hardships such as rain, hail, exhaustion, or altitude sickness, and perhaps get lost. The essential point is to have enough interest in spiritual practice to keep going despite its ups and downs. The satisfaction of making progress towards the goal you have set yourself will then be enough to nourish your determination and sustain your conviction that the effort is worthwhile.

Some General Advice

It is essential to maintain the continuity of meditation day after day, because in this way your practice can gradually gain substance and stability. This works just the same way as a small trickle of water that little by little turns into a stream and then a river. The traditional texts state that it is better to meditate regularly and repeatedly for short periods of time than to do long sessions every now and then. For example, you could devote twenty minutes a day to meditating formally and also take advantage of short breaks in your daily activities to call up the experience you had during your formal sessions again, even if only for a few moments.

Short regular sessions have a better chance of being high in quality than occasional long ones, and they will keep up a sense of continuity in your practice. For a plant to grow well, you have to water it a little every day. If you just pour a bucket of water on it once a month, it will most likely die between waterings. The same applies to meditation. This does not mean that you shouldn't occasionally meditate for longer periods if the opportunity arises.

If your meditation is too sporadic, there will be long periods during which you will fall back into your old habits and be overcome by negative emotions without being able to call on the support that meditation offers. But if you meditate frequently, even for short periods, it is possible to maintain a certain amount of your meditative experience between those formal sessions.

It is also said that being diligent in your practice should not depend on your mood of the moment. Whether your meditation session is enjoyable or irritating, easy or hard, the important point is to persevere. If you get bored while meditating, this is not due to meditation itself but to lack of training. Moreover, it is when you don't feel like meditating that it might have the most beneficial effects, because at those times meditation is working directly against some obstacle that stands in the way of your spiritual progress.

As we shall see later on when we look into this subject in detail, it is also important to keep your efforts balanced so that you don't become too loose or too tight. The Buddha had a student who was a great musician. He played the vina, a stringed instrument that resembles the sitar. This student had a lot of trouble meditating, and he questioned the Buddha about it. 'Sometimes,' he said, 'I make an intense effort to concentrate, and then I become too tense and tight. At other times, I try to loosen up, but then I get too relaxed and fall into a sluggish state. What should I do?' By way of response, the Buddha asked him, 'When you tune your instrument, what amount of tension do you put on the strings to make them sound the best?' The musician replied, 'They have to be neither too tight nor too loose.' The Buddha concluded: 'It's the same with meditation. For it to progress harmoniously, you must find the right balance between effort and relaxation.'

Practitioners are also advised not to place too much importance on various inner experiences that might arise in the course of meditation. Such experiences might take the form of bliss, inner clarity or an absence of thoughts. They can be compared to the different landscapes you see going by as you're sitting on a train. You would never consider getting off the train every time you noticed an interesting landscape, because the important thing is to keep going until you reach your destination. In the case of meditation, your goal is to transform yourself over the course of months and years. The progress you make is usually hardly noticeable from day to day, like the hands of a clock you hardly see moving. You have to be diligent but not impatient. Haste and meditation do not go together; any profound transformation is bound to take time. It doesn't matter if the way is long; there's no point in setting a deadline. The important thing is to know that you are heading in the right direction. Moreover, spiritual progress is not an all-or-nothing affair. Each step along the way, each stage, brings its measure of satisfaction and contributes towards your development. In essence, what matters is not occasionally to have some transitory experience but to see, after a few months or years of practice, that you have undergone a genuine and lasting change.

Turning the Mind Towards Meditation

In order to strengthen our determination to meditate, there are four points we should think about:

1. The preciousness of human life.
2. The fragility of human life and the transitoriness of all things.
3. The distinction between beneficial and harmful deeds.
4. The unsatisfactory quality inherent in many of the situations of life.

The Preciousness of Human Life

If we enjoy a minimum of freedom and opportunity, human life has extraordinary possibilities for inner development. Made use of intelligently, this life offers a unique opportunity to develop and actualize the potential we all possess but are so ready to neglect and fritter away. This potential, veiled by ignorance or mental confusion and by afflictive emotions, remains for the most part buried within us like a hidden treasure. The good qualities we acquire as we travel along the spiritual path represent the gradual emergence of this potential. This has been compared to a nugget of gold being cleaned – once the dirt has been removed, it shines with dazzling brilliance.

Meditation

Realize how precious human life is and arouse a deep wish to draw out its quintessential qualities. Compared to the life of animals, this human life offers you an extraordinary opportunity to accomplish good things on a scale beyond that of your own personal existence. Your human intelligence is an extremely powerful tool that can create great benefits or horrible disasters. Use it to achieve the gradual elimination of suffering and to discover genuine happiness, not only for yourself but also for those around you. In this way, every moment that passes will be worth living and you will have no regrets at the time of death, like a farmer who has cultivated his fields to the best of his ability. Remain for a few moments in this state of profound appreciation.

The Transitory Nature of All Things

What is the point of reflecting on the transitory nature of beings and things? Human life has incalculable value, but it doesn't last for ever. Reflecting on impermanence makes us realize the value of time. Each moment of life is so precious! Yet ordinarily we let it slip away like gold dust between our fingers. Why do we constantly put off until later what we intuitively know is of the highest importance? There's no point in jumping up and down with impatience to get results as fast as possible, but we do need to develop an unshakeable determination not to waste our time on distractions that make no sense. We must stop being taken in by the illusion that we have our whole life before us. Every moment of this life is precious, because death could occur at any time.

The way we think about death can exercise considerable

influence on the quality of our lives. Some people are terrified by death, others prefer not to think about it, still others contemplate it in order to appreciate the value of each passing moment and realize that it is worth living. We are all equals in the face of inevitable death, but we differ in the way we prepare for it and in the way we go through it. The sage relates to death as a reminder that arouses his courage and keeps him from vain distractions. He is not haunted by death, but he remains aware of the fragility of life. In this way, he gives full value to the time that is left to him. A person who takes advantage of every moment of his or her life to become a better person, one who is better able to contribute to the happiness of others, can die in peace.

If we realize the fundamentally changing nature of all things, how can we believe that any being is fundamentally good or bad, or that anything is permanently desirable or hateful? How can we perceive anything as intrinsically 'mine'? How can we conceive of a permanent self in the midst of the constantly changing stream of our consciousness?

Understanding that change is inherent in the nature of

all the animate or inanimate phenomena of the world keeps us from clinging to things as though they were going to last for ever. Such an attitude of clinging will sooner or later translate into suffering because it is out of step with reality. Moreover, when change does happen, we will be less shocked because we will realize that it is in the very nature of things, and we will find it less of an ordeal.

Meditation

Contemplate the passage of the seasons, of the days and months, of each moment, and the changes that affect every aspect of the life of beings. Then think about death, which is inevitable but whose time is uncertain. Who knows how much time you have left to live? Even if you live into old age, the latter part of your life will pass just as fast as the beginning, if not faster. So you need to consider, in the deepest part of yourself, what really counts in this life and use the time left to you to live in the most fruitful way possible — for your own sake and that of others. If you have the wish to meditate and develop your inner qualities, it is never too soon to start.

Sources of Inspiration

With all its many risks, this life endures
No more than wind-blown bubbles in a stream.
How marvellous to breathe in and out again,
To fall asleep and then awake refreshed.

—*Nagarjuna*[16]

In the beginning, you should be pursued by the fear of death like a deer escaping from a trap. In the middle, you should have nothing to regret, like a farmer who has tilled his field with care. In the end, you should be happy, like someone who has accomplished a great task.

—*Gampopa*

Behaviour That Should Be Cultivated and Behaviour That Should Be Refrained From

How can we make the best of this human life, which is precious but subject to being interrupted at any moment? If we want to carry out a plan or undertake some new activity, we have to be sure we are going about it in the right way. Certain things have to be done and others avoided. The sailor on the sea, the mountain guide or the conscientious craftsman all know that if they act according to the whim of the moment, nothing good will come of it. This is even more true if the goal we are pursuing is to liberate ourselves from suffering. The point here is not to set up good versus evil in some dogmatic fashion or to conform to some established convention.

Very simply, what we do have to do is behave with clear understanding and respect for the mechanisms of happiness and suffering that we ourselves can observe if we are attentive and insightful enough. It's as simple as realizing that if we keep our hand in the fire, there is no hope of escaping being burned. However, trying to be 100 per cent sure of the outcome of our choices is not a wise approach either. It is difficult to predict all the consequences of our deeds. But the least we can do — whatever activity we are involved in and whatever our circumstances may be — is to examine our motivation to be sure that our goal is not only of benefit to ourselves but also, and especially, of benefit to others.

Meditation

Let your mind rest in its natural state and clear your thoughts. Recognize how deeply you wish to be free from suffering and experience genuine happiness. Be intently aware that all living beings have the same wish. Reflect on the chains of causality that make certain types of thoughts, words and actions, for example, those inspired by hatred, greed, jealousy or pride, result in suffering, and then on those other chains of causality arising from benevolence and wisdom which lead to profound contentment. Take advantage of the wisdom of past teachers who have understood with great insight the mechanisms of happiness and suffering. Draw your conclusions as to what you should or should not do and arouse the determination to apply those conclusions in practice.

Source of Inspiration

For beings long to free themselves from misery,
But misery itself they follow and pursue.

They long for joy, but in their ignorance,
Destroy it, as they would a hated enemy.

—*Shantideva*[17]

The Unsatisfactory Quality Inherent in the Ordinary World

We have already seen that our situation is far from satisfactory and that transformation is not only desirable but also possible. We can try to distract ourselves in many ways from the unsatisfactory aspects of life or to disguise them in all kinds of attractive ways – for example, through engaging in endless activities, submerging ourselves in sensory experience or by pursuing wealth, power and fame. But reality, with its measure of suffering, will always confront us in the end. For this reason it is better to look reality in the face from the start and resolve to uproot the actual causes of suffering and cultivate the actual causes of genuine happiness.

Meditation

For a few moments, be aware of your potential for change. Whatever your present situation is, evolution and transformation are always possible. At the least, you can change your way of seeing things and then, gradually, your way of being as well. Resolve deep within to liberate yourself from your present situation and arouse the enthusiasm and the perseverance necessary to develop the good qualities that are latent within you.

Source of Inspiration

Spending all your life trying to achieve ordinary worldly goals [like pleasure, gain, praise and renown]... would be like trying to net fish in a dry riverbed. Clearly understanding this, make a firm decision not to allow your life to pursue such a useless course.

—Dilgo Khyentse Rinpoche[18]

Mindfulness Meditation

Our minds often get carried away with all kinds of thought associations in which dwelling on the past and projecting into the future are all mixed up. We become distracted, scattered, confused and therefore remote from the immediate reality before us. We are hardly aware of what is going on in the present moment – of the world around us, of our sensations or how our thoughts proliferate. In particular, we lose sight of the basic awareness that always lies behind these thought processes. Our automatic, mechanical thought patterns are the furthest thing from mindfulness. Mindfulness consists in being fully aware moment by moment of everything that arises within and around us – aware of everything we see, hear, feel or think. It also includes an *understanding* of the nature of our perceptions, free from the distortions that cause us to be attracted to them or to reject them. In addition, mindfulness contains an *ethical component* that enables us to discern whether or not it is beneficial to maintain this or that particular state of mind or to continue to pursue whatever we are doing at the present moment.

The past no longer exists, the future hasn't arisen yet and the present is paradoxically simultaneously ungraspable, for it never stays still and unchanging because, as a famous physicist once said, 'The present is the only thing that has no end.' Cultivating mindfulness does not mean that you should not take into account the lessons of the past or make plans for the future; rather it is a matter of living clearly in the present experience that includes them.

Meditation One

Observe what arises in your experience without imposing anything on it, without letting yourself be drawn to it or put off by it. See whatever is in front of you, a flower or any other object; listen attentively to the sounds nearby or far away; smell the fragrances and odours; feel the texture of what you are touching. Register your various sensations, clearly perceiving their characteristics. Be entirely present in what you are doing, whether you are walking, sitting down, writing, doing the dishes or drinking a cup of tea. Here there are no longer any pleasant or unpleasant tasks, because for mindfulness it doesn't matter what you are doing. What matters is how you do it, which should be with a mental presence that is clear and peaceful, that is attentive to and full of wonder at the present moment, yet still avoids adding your mental constructs on to reality.

When you are doing this practice, you stop endlessly flitting back and forth between attraction and rejection. You are just attentive, lucid, aware of each perception and sensation, of each thought that arises and passes away. Feel the freshness of the present moment. Do you find that this brings up a vast, luminous and serene state of mind in you?

Source of Inspiration

When you hear a sound during meditation, pay attention to the experience of hearing. That and only that... No mind movies. No concepts. No interior dialogues about the question. Just noise.

Reality is elegantly simple and unadorned. When you hear a sound, be mindful of the process of hearing. Everything else is just added chatter. Drop it.

—*Bhante Henepola Gunaratna*[19]

Meditation Two: Mindful Walking

Here is a method for cultivating mindfulness that is practised by many meditators. It consists of walking while concentrating totally on every step you take. You need to walk slowly enough to be able to be mindful of your least movement, but not so slowly that you lose your balance. With each step, be mindful of your balance, of how you touch your heel to the ground and then progressively bring your whole foot down, and of how the other foot comes off the ground and comes down again further on. Keep your gaze directed downward a few steps in front of you, maintaining the walking itself as your main object of concentration. If you don't have a big space, then walk back and forth, pausing for a second or two each time you turn round and remaining mindful of this interruption of your movement.

You may also combine walking with mindfulness of everything you encounter, that you see, hear and feel.

Source of Inspiration

Walking just for the pleasure of walking, freely and firmly, without hurrying. We are present in every step. When we wish to speak, we stop walking and lend all our attention to the person before us, to speaking and to listening… Stop, look around, and see how wonderful life is: the trees, the white clouds, the infinite sky. Listen to the birds, delight in the light breeze. Let us walk as free people and feel our steps growing lighter as we walk. Let us appreciate every step we take.

—*Thich Nhat Hanh*[20]

Inner Calm

The goal of meditation is to liberate the mind from ignorance and suffering. How do we do that? As stated above, just wishing will not make it so. We have to apply a systematic method that will free our mind from the veils that obscure it. Since it is the mind itself that has to do the job, first we have to prepare it properly. If it can't hold still for a minute, how can it free itself from its own ignorance? The situation is like that of a monkey, an analogy used earlier. In this case the monkey is tethered by numerous ropes and continually jumps about in all directions trying to get loose. He jumps around so much that neither he nor anybody who wants to help him can untie a single knot. So the first thing that has to be done is to calm him down and make him pay attention. Calming the monkey doesn't mean forcibly holding him still while keeping him tied up. The goal here is to profit from a moment of calm to free him. In the same way we must take advantage of the respite that comes with a relatively calm, clear and workable mind to free it from the bonds created by wild thoughts, conflicting emotions and confusion.

The obstacles to attaining this goal are automatic thought patterns perpetuated by our habitual tendencies and the distractions and fabrications of the conceptual mind that distort reality. Thus we have to overcome these unfavourable conditions. Mastering the mind does not mean imposing an additional set of constraints on it that will make it even more tense and cramped than it already is. What it means is just the opposite – freeing it from the constraints of mental conditioning and inner conflicts created by dysfunctional thoughts and emotions.

So, in order to recognize the fundamental nature of the mind, we have to remove the veils created by automatic thought patterns. How do we do that? Let's say we are trying to get back a key that has fallen in a pond. If we take a stick and poke about on the bottom, we'll completely muddy the water and won't have the slightest chance of spotting the key. The first thing we have to do is let the water settle until it becomes clear. After that, it will be easy to see the key and retrieve it. We must work with our mind in the same way. We have to begin by getting it clear, calm and attentive. After that we can use this new skill to cultivate other qualities like altruistic love and compassion as well as developing a deeper insight into the nature of mind.

In all schools of Buddhism, two basic complementary types of meditation are practised to attain these goals. One is 'calm abiding', *shamatha* in Sanskrit, the other is 'deeper insight', *vipashyana* in Sanskrit. *Shamatha* is a peaceful state of mind, clear and perfectly concentrated on its object. *Vipashyana* is the deep insight into the nature of the mind and of the phenomenal world. We acquire this deep insight first by detailed analysis of consciousness and then through contemplation, that is, through inner experience. *Vipashyana* allows us to see through illusion so we can cease to be a victim of afflictive emotions. In essence, *shamatha* prepares the ground by making the mind into a manageable tool that is precise and effective; *vipashyana* then liberates the mind from the yoke of mental afflictions and the veils of ignorance.

Most of the time our mind is unstable, whim driven and disorderly, and it bounces back and forth between hope and fear. It is self-centred, hesitant, fragmented, confused, sometimes even absent, as well as weakened by internal contradictions and a feeling of insecurity. On top of that, it rebels against any kind of training, and is constantly occupied by a kind of inner chatter that keeps up a background noise we are barely aware of. These dysfunctional states are nothing more than products of the mind itself. Therefore it is only logical that it is possible for the mind itself to remedy them. That is the object of practising *shamatha* and *vipashyana*.

So the idea is to gradually progress from a state of mind where the unfavourable conditions just described prevail, to another state that is characterized by stable attention, inner peace and clarity, confidence, courage, openness towards others, benevolence, the ability to deal with emotions and other qualities of a vast and calm mind.

In the beginning the practice of *shamatha* works to pacify the turbulence of our thoughts. In order to do that, we sharpen our powers of concentration by using the support of something we rarely pay any attention to – the coming and going of our breath.

Normally – unless we are out of breath from some

effort or have been holding our breath — we are hardly aware of the coming and going of the breath. This is true despite the fact that breathing is almost synonymous with being alive. Since our breathing just goes on by itself, if we can use it as a support for our concentration, we will have a tool that is precious because it is always available, and which, in addition, can play the role of a reference point in gauging concentration or distraction.

This practice has three essential stages:

1. Directing the attention to a chosen object (in this case the breath).
2. Maintaining the attention on this object.
3. Being mindful of the characteristics of the object.[21]

Meditation: Mindfulness of the Breath

Sit in a comfortable position. If possible, adopt the seven-point posture described earlier on pages 49–52, or at least take a position in which you are erect and well balanced. Here, mindfulness consists of remaining continuously aware of your breathing without forgetting it or letting yourself be distracted.

Breathe calmly and naturally. Concentrate all your attention on the coming and going of the breath. More specifically, focus your attention on the sensation created by the passage of air through your nostrils, the place where you perceive it most acutely. The precise spot varies from person to person: it might be at the opening of the nostrils, a little further inside, or higher up in the sinuses. Also notice the moment when breathing is suspended — between the out-breath and the following in-breath. After that, concentrate again on the point where you feel the breath passing. Then also note the point when the breath halts for a moment, between the in-breath and the following out-breath.

Stay concentrated in the same way during the next cycle of breathing, breath after breath, without getting tense but also without relaxing to the point of falling into a sluggish state. Your awareness of the breath should be clear and calm. The Buddha gave the example of a cloud of dust raised by the wind. The dust was dispelled by a rain shower, giving way to a pure and brilliant sky. The dust here is the agitation and confusion of the mind; concentration on the breath is the saving rain shower; and the pure sky is calm and inner clarity.

Avoid intentionally altering the rhythm of your breath. Your breathing will probably slow a little, but that should be allowed to happen naturally. Whether your breath is long or short, simply be aware of the fact that it *is* long or short.

Sooner or later you will wander into a state of distraction accompanied by a lot of thoughts, into a vague sleepy state or even a combination of both, that is, into a state of confusion marked by erratic thought associations. It is at this point that vigilance has to be applied. As soon as you notice that you have lost your concentration, just resume it, without adding to your distraction by feeling regret or guilt. Noticing that you have been distracted already marks the return of your mindfulness. Just come back to the breath, like a butterfly coming back to a flower after having fluttered around here and there for no apparent reason.

When thoughts appear, don't try to block them,

which is not possible anyway because they are already there, just avoid feeding them. Let them pass through the field of your awareness the way a bird passes through the sky without leaving a trace.

Occasionally, you can also take the distraction itself as the object of your mindfulness. Then, once your mind has become attentive again, return your attention to the breath.

If other physical sensations appear, for example, pain from sitting in the same position for a long time, do not rebel against the pain or become overwhelmed by it. Include it in your mindfulness, and then return to observing your breath. If the pain becomes so acute that it disturbs your meditation, it is a good idea to relax your position for a few moments or practise mindful walking for a short time. Then resume your meditation on the breath with a fresh mind and renewed concentration.

Variation One

One method for reviving your concentration when it has become too weak is to count your breath. For example, you can mentally count 'one' at the end of a complete out-breath in-breath cycle, then 'two' at the end of the next cycle, and so on up to ten. Then begin again with 'one'. This will help maintain your concentration.

If you prefer, you can also count 'one' at the end of an in-breath and 'two' at the end of the following out-breath. This method and the ones that follow can be applied from time to time whenever it seems helpful, but it is not necessary to count your breath during your whole meditation.

Variation Two

Another method is to mentally repeat 1, 1, 1, 1, 1... fairly rapidly during the course of an in-breath, then 2, 2, 2, 2, 2... in the same way during the course of the next out-breath. For the next cycle, count 3, 3, 3, 3, 3... during the in-breath and 4, 4, 4, 4, 4... during the out-breath. Count that way up to ten, then start a new series.

Another possibility is to count rapidly from one to ten during the in-breath and then do the same during the out-breath. The object of these various ways of counting the breath is to refresh your concentration when it becomes sluggish or distracted.

Variation Three

Instead of observing the breath itself, you may concentrate on feeling the up and down movement of the abdomen that accompanies your breathing.

Variation Four

You can also associate a simple phrase with the coming and going of the breath. For example, while breathing out, you can mentally say, 'May all beings be happy,' and while breathing in, 'May all their suffering be dispelled.'

Variation Five

Practitioners who recite mantras can combine silent recitation with attention to the breath. Thus with 'om mani padme hum',[22] which is the mantra of the Buddha of Compassion (Avalokiteshvara in Sanskrit), you say 'om' while breathing in, 'mani padme' while holding the breath for a brief moment, and 'hum' while breathing out.

Variation Six

Normally, you should not influence the movement of the breath nor slow down at the transitional point between in-breaths and out-breaths, but in this variant you concentrate for a few instants on the pause in breathing as the breath dissipates at the end of an out-breath. This is also the point at which discursive thoughts are suspended for a few instants. During this brief moment, rest in this clear bright space, calm and free from mental fabrications. You should not, however, conceptualize this experience. Just recognize it is a basic aspect of your mind that is always present behind the curtain of thoughts.

These different variations can be practised as you choose in order to improve your concentration.

The Four Foundations of Mindfulness

The following meditations are intended to cultivate mindfulness and help develop a clearer understanding of the nature of mind and phenomena. You will successively focus your attention on your body, feelings, mind and on phenomena at large (anything that is experienced).

Meditation One: Mindfulness of the Body

Adopt a comfortable, relaxed posture and direct your awareness to your body. When walking, be aware that you are walking; when standing, be aware that you are standing; when sitting, be aware that you are sitting; when lying down, be aware that you are lying down. Be aware of bending down or straightening up, bending forwards or backwards, lowering or lifting your head, eating, drinking and so on.

You can also be mindful of your breath, as described earlier.

Then, concentrate on the various parts of your body, one after the other. Begin with your head, hair, ears, eyes, mouth, teeth, etc. Go down along your neck, shoulders, arms, hands and fingernails. Move to the chest, the waist, going down to the sole of your feet. Go up again.

Then visualize the inside of your body: the flesh, the tendons, the bones, the heart, the lungs, the veins and arteries and the blood running through them, the other bodily fluids, the liver and the intestines, and focus your mindfulness on them.

Finally, simple place your awareness on whichever perception of the body arises in your mind.

Meditation Two: Mindfulness of Feelings

Whenever you perceive any feeling, whether pleasant, unpleasant or neutral, simply embrace it with your awareness. Feel the breeze passing on your face, the touch between your two hands or the point of contact of your feet with the ground.

If the feeling is pleasant simply be aware of its pleasantness; if it is unpleasant be aware of its unpleasantness. In the latter case, for instance, the sheer awareness of the unpleasantness replaces the reaction of rejection that usually takes place.

If you experience a diffuse feeling of your inner organs, concentrate on that. You may also concentrate on some parts of the body where you may not have any particular sensation at the moment, like your forehead or ears. Become aware of the subtle feeling of their presence.

Finally, try to investigate the very nature of feelings. Aren't they just movements of the mind? Isn't it the same awareness that perceives them all without being affected by them?

Meditation Three: Mindfulness of Mind
When thoughts arise, whether you follow after them or try to chase them, you often feel overwhelmed by them. Instead, simply be aware of your thoughts and watch them like a spectator.

Whether your mind enters a state of craving, resentment or confusion, whether it is focused or scattered, dull or lucid, calm or agitated, be mindful of these states.

As will be explained later, you will also need to understand the nature of these thoughts and find ways to free yourself from afflictive mental states.

Meditation Four: Mindfulness of Phenomena

Be fully aware of whatever comes into the field of your experience and becomes an object for your mind: forms, sounds, odours, tastes, textures, thoughts, emotions – joy, sadness, desire, fear, irritation, dullness and so on.

Whatever arises becomes a support for your meditation. Watch how these phenomena appear, remain for a while and vanish. Reflect on their transitory and illusory nature.

When your mind jumps from one phenomenon to another – sounds, forms, smells, etc. – and many thoughts flash through your mind in quick succession, if you remain mindful, the objects that attract your attention and thoughts themselves may change, but you will be able to achieve a continuous, all-pervading, panoramic mindfulness.

Concentration on an Object

There are many other ways to cultivate concentration and mental calm. These methods are of two kinds — with or without an object of concentration. The object of concentration can be the coming and going of the breath, as I described earlier, but your attention can also be placed on other physical sensations, on an external object, on an emotion or on a visualized image. The external object can be a completely ordinary one, such as a small stone, a flower or a candle flame. As with the breathing, the training consists in letting the mind rest attentively on the chosen object, bringing it back to this object when you notice you have become distracted.

The object can also be a symbolic or figurative image associated with a spiritual path, for example, for those who are practising the Buddhist path, a painting or statue of the Buddha. You begin by concentrating on the external representation long enough so that all its details are present in your mind. Then concentrate on the mental image of the external representation. The following is the synopsis of an instruction given by Dilgo Khyentse Rinpoche.

Meditation

Sit down and assume the seven-point posture. Let your mind calm down for a few moments and then visualize Buddha Shakyamuni in the space in front of you. He is seated on a moon disk, which is resting on a lotus and a throne held up by eight lions. His body is resplendent, like a mountain of gold. With his right hand, he touches the ground next to his right knee in the gesture of taking the earth to witness. His left hand rests in his lap in the gesture of equanimity and holds a begging bowl filled with nectar. He wears the three monastic robes, and from his body emanates infinite rays of light and wisdom that fill the universe. Bring this image to life. Imagine that the Buddha you have visualized is not inert like a drawing or a statue. It is not made of flesh and blood either: his body is luminous and transparent like a rainbow, radiant with wisdom and compassion.

Try to concentrate one-pointedly on this complete visualization. You may then turn your attention to the details, to the perfect oval of the face, to the eyes filled with wisdom and love, on the harmoniously proportioned nose and ears, on the smile, on the rays of light streaming out from the body. Progressively extend your concentration to all the details of the Buddha's form from top to bottom and from bottom to top, giving it the same level of meticulous attention a painter would give. Again, visualize the whole form of the Buddha, while retaining each detail as distinctly as possible

To reinforce your concentration, immediately neutralize anything that might disturb your mind. If your thoughts get agitated so that they keep you from developing a clear image, slightly lower your gaze (which normally rests in space) and concentrate on the lower part of the Buddha: the crossed legs, the throne held up by the lions or the lotus seat. The effect of that will be to reduce your mental agitation.

If your mind falls into a state of sluggishness, slackness or dull indifference, raise your eyes and concentrate on the upper part of the visualization: the Buddha's face, his eyes, the point between his eyebrows.

If your visualization is not clear, don't give up but keep trying to get it more refined and precise. If it is clear, hold it in a natural way without tension.

When your mind becomes stable and peaceful, examine it. Realize that the image you are visualizing is not the Buddha himself but a projection of your mind whose goal is to help you cultivate concentration. Even though your mind has the ability to concentrate on an object, the mind itself cannot be found anywhere. It is impossible to locate mind, to identify its shape, colour or form, or to see where it comes from, where it stays or where it is going. You will never find anything. The mind is not an independent entity that can be identified as such.

The same is true of the body. What we call 'the body' is simply a conglomeration of many elements put together. We give the name 'heap' to a collection of grains, 'sheaf' to a collection of dried straw, and 'crowd' to a gathering of people, but none of them are entities in their own right. Likewise for this collection of things we call the body, if you take away the skin and the flesh, the marrow, the bones and the different organs, once they have all been separated from each other there is no other entity present that you can identify as 'the body'.

In fact, all phenomena in their infinite variety throughout the universe, appear as a result of particular causes and conditions coming temporarily together. You take phenomena to be things that truly exist simply because you have not examined them properly. In truth, they have no solid intrinsic existence at all.

When it becomes clear that your body, the image of the Buddha you are visualizing, and all phenomena are the display of the mind and that the mind's nature is not an entity endowed with independent existence but rather a dynamic stream of experiences, simply remain in the recognition of that nature without wandering. Remain attentive to whether or not thoughts interrupt this recognition. When thoughts arise, be aware of them without either hindering or encouraging them. This is what is called 'deep insight'. It is essential to bring together mental calm, *shamatha*, and deep insight, *vipashyana*, in this way.

Source of Inspiration

Flawless *shamatha* is like an oil-lamp that is unmoved by wind. Wherever the attention is placed, it is unwaveringly present; awareness is vividly clear, without being sullied by laxity, lethargy, or dimness; wherever the awareness is directed, it is steady and sharply pointed; unmoved by adventitious thoughts, it is straight. In this way, a flawless meditative state arises in one's mind-stream; and until this happens, it is important that the mind is settled in its natural state.

—*Padmasambhava*[23]

Concentration Without an Object

At first, it might seem that meditation without an object would be easier than meditation with an object. But, in fact, it is harder to keep your mind clear and concentrated on itself in a state of pure awareness than to concentrate on something. Concentration on an object implies a certain mental activity connected with attention, and even if it is hard to maintain this concentration, it is nevertheless easier than resting your mind in a state of perfect simplicity devoid of all mental constructs. That being said, you should know that concentration without an object is the natural culmination of concentration with an object and represents a further step in the understanding of the basic nature of the mind through direct experience.

Meditation

Direct your mind inward and allow it to contemplate its primary quality, which is simply *knowing*. This faculty of knowing – which is mindfulness in its pure state – illuminates all thoughts and all perceptions. It is a constant and fundamental quality of the flow of consciousness. You can experience it even in the absence of thoughts and mental images. Try to identify this primordial aspect of all experience, and then let your mind rest a few moments in this non-dual awareness that is clear, lucid and devoid of concepts and discursive thoughts.

Source of Inspiration

It is present as transparent, utter openness.

Without outside, without inside,

An all-pervasiveness

Without boundary and without direction.

The wide-open expanse of the view,

The true condition of mind,

Is like sky, like space

Without centre, without edge, without aim.

—*Shabkar*[24]

Overcoming Obstacles

Any training requires effort, and any change naturally encounters resistance. In the case of training the mind and of non-conceptual meditation, there are various obstacles that can slow your progress. Included among the obstacles discussed in traditional instructions on meditation are sluggishness and its opposite, distracted agitation, as well as the lack of perseverance and its opposite, excessive effort.

Laziness, usually interpreted as indolence or lack of motivation, can take several forms. Ordinary laziness is the fault of shying away from any effort. Its antidote consists of recalling the preciousness of human existence and of each passing moment and contemplating the benefits of inner transformation. Reflecting on those themes allows you to rekindle your inspiration and enthusiasm.

Another form of laziness is thinking: 'That's not for me; it's beyond my abilities. I'd rather not get involved with it.' In other words, you give up the race before you reach the starting line. To overcome this obstacle, give the potential for transformation that exists in you its true value and look at the object of life on a larger scale.

A third form of laziness is not having the determination to do immediately what you know to be the most important thing and wasting your time instead on minor activities. To remedy this, establish priorities among your projects, and remember that while your days are numbered, ordinary activities are like waves on the ocean – there is no end to them.

DISTRACTION

This is the most common of meditation's enemies. What practitioner is not the victim of it? Distraction is completely normal, because when you begin to practise, your mind is undisciplined and chaotic and you can't reasonably expect it to calm down immediately – so there is no reason to give up hope. The goal of meditation is precisely to make your mind smooth and manageable so that it can be concentrated or relaxed at will; and especially to free it from the tyranny of mental afflictions and confusion. The antidote to distraction is cultivating vigilance. Whenever you notice that your mind has wandered off, bring it back to the object of meditation. If you suddenly realize you have been distracted, it shows you have recovered your mindfulness, so you should be happy about this instead of being discouraged and regretful. The more often you *notice* that you have been distracted, the more your mindfulness is progressing. Remember also why you are meditating. Your goal is not to waste time giving free rein to your thoughts, but to use your meditation time to gain freedom from suffering.

These are also major obstacles that make us lose the thread of meditation. Sluggishness, or laxity, undermines the clarity of the mind; agitation undermines its stability. The former can range from simple heaviness to sleep, with lethargy, irritation, daydreaming or other vague and blurry mental states in between. The mind withdraws and becomes excessively inward. This kind of lack of clarity is a major obstacle precisely because you want to use your concentration to better understand the nature of the mind. As Bokar Rinpoche, a contemporary meditation master, explains: 'When we look at the sea in the full light of day, we can see stones and algae on the bottom through the clear water. Meditation should have this same clarity, which allows us to be mindfully aware of the situation of our mind. By night, on the other hand, the surface of the waves is a dark and opaque mass that our vision cannot penetrate; in this same way a dim and heavy mind, in spite of an appearance of stability, is a hindrance to meditating.'[25]

The advice for countering this state is to adopt a more upright and energetic posture, to gaze somewhat upwards into the space in front of you, and to wear less clothing if you are too warmly dressed. You should also refresh your attention, putting the emphasis on the mindfulness of the present moment.

Agitation is a hyperactive form of distraction in which the mind produces a chain of thoughts that is maintained by automatic patterns and imagination. This feverish agitation keeps transporting you far away from your object of concentration. Your body is sitting quietly, but your mind is taking a world tour. When this occurs, relax your physical posture a bit, lower your gaze and come back to yourself by recalling why you are there and what the goal of your efforts is.

LACK OF PERSEVERANCE AND EXCESSIVE EFFORT

Any kind of training requires regular effort. A lack of perseverance considerably diminishes the effects of meditation and thus reduces its power to transform us. As pointed out earlier, a big occasional effort does not have the same beneficial effect as less spectacular effort that is more constant. Sporadic efforts will not be enough to transform the mind in a deep and long-lasting way.

The remedy for this weakness is, again, to reflect on the preciousness of the time that is passing, on the uncertainty of the duration of life and on the benefits of the training you are engaged in.

You might also temporarily fall into the opposite fault of excessive effort by overdoing the remedies to laxity. The tension resulting from that also ends up as a distraction to your meditation. For this reason, you have to balance your efforts and find the happy medium between tension and relaxation, as the Buddha advised the *vina* player to do in the example given earlier. So stop applying a particular antidote when it is no longer necessary and let the mind rest calmly in its natural state.

Excessive effort can also result from impatience or exaltation, two states that lead nowhere. If you begin climbing a high mountain at a run, your lungs will soon force you to stop. In the same way, if you draw a bow too far, it will break, or if you try to cook on too high a flame, you will end up burning your food.

Demanding immediate results is an aspect of unsteadiness of mind or laziness. His Holiness the Dalai Lama jocularly remarked: 'In the West, people would like

enlightenment to be fast, easy and if possible...cheap!'
In the same way that it takes patience to grow a crop,
steadiness is indispensable for the practice of meditation.
It does no good to pull on your plants to make them
grow faster!

Nine Methods for Cultivating Attention

The traditional meditation texts teach nine methods to
help establish the mind in a state of equanimity and make
it more stable. Bear in mind that here I am talking about
mindfulness as remaining continually attentive to a
chosen object of concentration:

1. Focus your mind, even if at the beginning it is only
   for a brief moment, on an object, following the
   instructions, and avoid letting your mind be
   carried away by images and discursive thoughts.
2. Refocus your mind repeatedly, asking yourself
   again and again, 'Am I keeping my attention on
   the object?' Bring it back quickly to its object
   as soon as you notice distraction has caused it to

stray. To do that, you first have to recognize that your mind has been distracted, identify the emotion or thought that has brought about this distraction, and apply the appropriate antidote. Little by little, you will develop the ability to keep your mind calm and stable for longer periods of time and your concentration will become clearer and clearer.

3. Keep your mind on this object continuously over a longer period of time, without falling into distraction. In order to do this, focus on the instructions for maintaining concentration on the mind's support on pages 80–83. Recall those instructions and apply them with care. If you do this, you will be able to recognize distraction almost as soon as it occurs.

4. Direct your mind with care. The firmer your mind is and the more precise it is in its concentration, the more you will be inclined to meditate. Even if your attention is not yet perfect, you will reach the point where you no longer completely lose track of the object of meditation, and you will become free

from the coarsest and most disturbing forms of mental agitation.

5. Master your mind. Your concentration will become more stable, but you might fall into a subtle form of sluggishness or laxity. When your concentration deteriorates in this way, renew the sharpness and clarity of your awareness, and rekindle your inspiration and enthusiasm by considering the benefits of perfect concentration (*samadhi*).

6. Pacify your mind. Heightening your mindfulness to counteract subtle mental slackness may lead to subtle agitation. When your concentration becomes too sharp or is shaken by the subtle mental agitation that takes the form of a little conversation going on in the background of your attention, simply consider the drawbacks of agitation and distraction. This will calm your mind and make it clear and transparent like the pure sound of a well-tuned musical instrument.

7. Pacify your mind completely by using sustained

and energetic attention to abandon all attachment to meditative experiences that may arise. These experiences can appear in a number of forms, such as bliss, clarity or absence of discursive thoughts. They can also take the form of spontaneous bursts of joy, of unshakeable confidence, fear, exaltation, discouragement, certainty or doubt, renunciation of worldly concerns, passion, intense devotion or negative views. Any of these experiences can arise for no apparent reason. They are a sign of profound changes going on in your mind. It is necessary to keep yourself from identifying with these experiences and from attributing more importance to them than you would to the landscapes going by outside the train window. Perfectly pacified attention will cause these experiences to fade away without upsetting your mind. You will then know a profound inner peace.

8. Keep your attention concentrated on one point. After having eliminated sluggishness and mental

agitation, you will develop the ability to keep your attention stable and clear through an entire meditation session. Your mind will then be like a lamp protected from the wind, whose stable and bright flame gives out maximal light. A minimal effort at the beginning of the session will then be enough to establish the mind within the flow of concentration, where it can be maintained without difficulty, remaining in its natural state free from constraints and disturbances.

9. Rest in a state of perfect equilibrium. When your mind has become completely used to concentrating on a single point, it will remain in a state of equanimity that will arise spontaneously and perpetuate itself without effort.

The Development of Inner Calm

Gradually your mind will calm down. However, just the opposite may seem to be happening. When you try to calm your mind, it may seem that you have more thoughts than before. The truth is that they have not increased in number, but rather you have become aware of how many there are. I have already pointed out that it is neither possible nor desirable to block thoughts. It is important, however, to gain some mastery over the thought process if you want to eliminate the causes of suffering and make possible the development of genuine well-being. Automatic thought patterns only strengthen our dependence on the causes of suffering, while regular meditation, far from bringing about any kind of stupor or destroying spontaneity, leads to the freedom that comes with mastery of the mind and inner peace. The Buddhist texts illustrate the pacification of turbulent thoughts through the metaphor of a roaring waterfall that calms down gradually as its waters flow into the plains and finally run into the vast ocean. This meditative development occurs in five stages, which are portrayed in five images:

1. A waterfall tumbling from a cliff. Thoughts continuously add up and multiply. They seem more numerous than before because you are becoming aware of the movement of your mind.
2. A torrent hurtling through successive gorges.

The mind alternates between periods of rest and activity.

3. A broad river flowing with few obstructions. The mind becomes occasionally agitated when it is disturbed by significant events but otherwise remains calm.

4. A lake ruffled by a few waves. The mind is mildly agitated on the surface but remains calm and clear in the depths.

5. A peaceful ocean. Unshakeable and effortless concentration no longer requires antidotes against wandering thoughts.

Such a development is not accomplished in one day or even a few weeks but, sooner or later, the moment will come when you see real progress. We readily accept the idea that it takes time and perseverance to master an art, a sport, a language or any other discipline. Why should it not be the same with training the mind? It is a worthwhile adventure. We are not talking about acquiring some ordinary ability, but rather of acquiring mastery and a way of being that will determine the quality of our whole life.

Source of Inspiration

At the beginning, nothing comes.

In the middle, nothing remains.

In the end, nothing goes away.

—Milarepa

Meditations on Altruistic Love

We have all, to varying degrees, had the experience of profound altruistic love, of a feeling of all-encompassing benevolence, of intense compassion for those who are suffering. Some of us are naturally more altruistic than others, sometimes to the point of heroism. Others are more turned in on themselves and find it hard to consider the welfare of others as an essential goal, and even harder to put the welfare of others before their own. Whichever the case may be, it is essential to cultivate altruism. Being altruistic not only helps us to benefit others, but it is also the most satisfying way to live. This is the opposite of a heightened feeling of self-importance that only brings pain to oneself and others.

In general, even when altruistic thoughts arise in our mind, they are fairly quickly replaced by other less wholesome thoughts such as those of anger or jealousy. That is why, if we want altruism to play a major role in our being, we must spend some time cultivating it, because just wishing is not enough.

As we discussed earlier, meditation is a means of familiarizing ourselves with a new way of being. Now, how can we meditate on altruism? First of all, we must realize that in the deepest part of ourselves, we do not want to suffer, we want to aspire to happiness. Once we have recognized this aspiration, the next thing we have to do is realize that all beings share it. We also need to realize that the right not to suffer, though often ignored, is without a doubt the most fundamental right of all beings. Finally, we must realize that there are causes and conditions to suffering and therefore remedies to it.

Unfortunately, when it comes to choosing the means of creating happiness and preventing suffering, we are often unskilful or altogether off the mark. Some people get lost on the wrong track by blindly seeking to achieve their own happiness at the price of others' suffering. Generally speaking, we should unreservedly wish for all sentient beings to be delivered from the causes of suffering. To this end, the Buddhist texts advise us to cultivate four particular thoughts or attitudes and to expand them without limit. These are altruistic love, compassion, joy in the happiness of others, and impartiality.

Meditation One: Altruistic Love

Imagine that a young child approaches you and gives you a look that is joyous, confident and full of innocence. You stroke his head, look at him with tenderness, and take him in your arms. You feel a sense of unconditional benevolence and love. Let yourself be entirely pervaded by this love that wishes for nothing more than his well-being. Then, cultivate, sustain and nourish this feeling of loving kindness. When it declines, revive it. At the end of the session, rest for a few moments in the mindful awareness of love.

You could also choose someone else towards whom you feel great tenderness and deep gratitude. Wish with all your heart that this person will find happiness and the causes of happiness, and then extend this wish to all those you are close to, then to those you know less well, then progressively to all beings.

Finally, extend this wish to your personal enemies and to the enemies of all humanity. This last case obviously does not mean you wish them success in their deadly plans. You are simply formulating a strong wish that they will give up their hatred, greed, cruelty and indifference and that benevolence and care for the happiness of others will be born in their minds. The worse an illness is, the more need the sick person has for care, attention and goodwill.

In this way, embrace the totality of beings with a feeling of limitless love.

Meditation Two: Compassion

Now imagine that someone dear to you has been the victim of a terrible accident. It is night time, and she is lying covered with blood on the roadside, suffering from terrible pain. Help is late in arriving and you don't know what to do. You feel this dear person's suffering intensely, as though it was your own, and this is mixed with a growing sense of distress and helplessness. This pain strikes you in the deepest part of your being, to the point where it becomes nearly intolerable. What should you do?

At this moment, let yourself go into an immense feeling of love towards this person. Imagine taking her gently in your arms. Imagine that waves of love stream forth from you and pour over her. Imagine that each atom of her suffering is replaced by an atom of love. Wish from the bottom of your heart for her to survive, be healed and cease to suffer.

This feeling of compassion comes from the same place in you as altruistic love and is nothing else than love applied to suffering.

Now extend this compassion to other people who are close to you, then, little by little, to all beings, making the following wish deep in your heart: 'May all beings be free from suffering and the causes of suffering.'

Meditation Three: Rejoicing in the Happiness of Others

There are people in this world who have tremendously good qualities and others who lavish benefits on humanity and whose humanitarian projects have been crowned with success. There are also people who have realized their aspirations through great effort and steadfast perseverance, and still others who possess many talents.

Rejoice from the bottom of your heart in their accomplishments. Wish for their good qualities not to wane, but on the contrary to continue and flourish. The ability to feel joy in the most positive qualities of others is the best antidote there is to discouragement and to a dim and desperate view of the world and of human beings. It is also the remedy for envy and jealousy, which are reflections of the inability to rejoice in the happiness of others.

Meditation Four: Impartiality

Impartiality is an essential element in the three preceding meditations, because the wish for all beings to be delivered from suffering and its causes has to be universal and not dependent on our personal bias or on the way others treat us. Take the point of view of a doctor who takes it on himself to heal sick people no matter who they are or how seriously ill they are.

Realize that all beings, whether they are close to you, strangers or enemies, want to avoid suffering. Also reflect on the fundamental interdependence of all the phenomena of the universe and of the beings that inhabit it. Interdependence is the very basis of altruism. Like the sun that shines equally on good people and evil ones, on beautiful landscapes or dung heaps, do your best to extend the altruistic love, compassion and joy you cultivated in the three preceding meditations to all beings without distinction.

Recall again that when it comes to your own and others' enemies, you do not intend to encourage or passively tolerate their attitudes and harmful acts, but you look at them as very sick or mad people. So with the same goodwill that you feel towards those who are close to you, wish for the ignorance and destructive feelings that rule them to be eradicated from their consciousness.

Combining the Four Meditations

Begin with altruistic love, the strong wish for others to find happiness and the causes of happiness. If, after a while, this love drifts towards self-centred attachment, move on to the meditation on impartiality in order to extend your love and compassion equally to all beings – dear ones, strangers or enemies.

If your impartiality turns into indifference, it is time to think of people who are suffering and arouse intense compassion within you with the wish to relieve these beings from all their suffering. But it can happen that, as a result of being continually concerned with the endless misfortunes of others, you may be overcome by a feeling of depression and helplessness, even despair, to the point where you feel overwhelmed by the immensity of the task and lose heart. At that point meditate on your joy in the happiness of others, thinking of those people who possess great human qualities and of those people whose altruistic aspirations have been successful. Rejoice fully in that.

If that joy turns into blind euphoria and distraction, go back again to altruistic love – and so on. Develop the four thoughts in this way while avoiding the pitfalls possible in each of them.

At the end of your meditation, contemplate the interdependence of all things for a few moments and their lack of autonomous, intrinsic existence. Understand that, just as a bird needs two wings to fly, you must develop wisdom and compassion simultaneously. Wisdom is a better understanding of reality and compassion is the desire for all beings to be liberated from the causes of suffering.

Sources of Inspiration

Compassion is a spontaneous feeling of connection with all living things. What you feel, I feel; what I feel, you feel. There's no difference between us… When I began to practise meditation on compassion, however, I found that my sense of isolation began to diminish, while at the same time my personal sense of empowerment began to grow. Where once I saw only problems, I started to see solutions. Where once

I viewed my own happiness as more important than the happiness of others, I began to see the well-being of others as the foundation of my own peace of mind.

—*Yongey Mingyur Rinpoche*[26]

May I be a guard for those who are protectorless,
A guide for those who journey on the road.
For those who wish to go across the water,
May I be a boat, a raft, a bridge.

May I be an isle for those who yearn for landfall,
And a lamp for those who long for light;
For those who need a resting-place, a bed;
For all who need a servant, may I be their slave.

May I be the wishing jewel, the vase of plenty,
A word of power and the supreme healing,
May I be the tree of miracles,
And for every being the abundant cow.

Like the earth and the pervading elements,
Enduring as the sky itself endures,

For boundless multitudes of living beings,

May I be their ground and sustenance.

Thus for every thing that lives,

As far as are the limits of the sky,

May I provide their livelihood and nourishment

Until they pass beyond the bonds of suffering.

—*Shantideva*[27]

As long as space endures,

As long as there are beings to be found,

May I continue likewise to remain

To drive away the sorrows of the world.

—*Shantideva*[28]

A Sublime Exchange

Profound suffering can sometimes awaken our hearts and minds and open them to others. There is a particular practice whose purpose is to turn this opening into a lasting state. It consists of mentally exchanging the suffering of others for our own happiness and also in wishing that our own suffering may stand for the suffering of others. This is done through the vehicle of the breath.

Perhaps we think we have enough problems already and it's asking too much to add to our burden by taking on the suffering of others. However, what happens as a result of this practice is just the opposite. Experience shows that when we mentally take on, transform and dissolve the suffering of others through compassion, not only does that not increase our own suffering but it dispels it. The reason for this is that altruistic love and compassion are the most powerful antidotes there are to our own pain. So this is a situation where everybody wins! On the other

hand, self-centred dwelling on our suffering, reinforced by the constant refrain of 'me, me, me' that it causes to resonate in our head, undermines our courage and increases our distress. But by breaking the spell of our self-centredness, altruistic contemplation of the suffering of others greatly enhances our compassionate courage and our resolve to dispel their suffering.

This practice of exchange is a particularly effective means of developing altruism and compassion through meditation. As a result of it, when we actually come face to face with the suffering of others, we will be naturally inclined to behave in a compassionate manner and offer to help.

Meditation

Begin by feeling a strong sense of altruistic love towards a person who has been very good to you – your mother, for example. Think about her kindness. She gave you life after having gone through the difficulties of pregnancy and the pains of childbirth. As you grew up, she took care of you without sparing her strength. She put your happiness before her own and was always ready to sacrifice everything for you.

In order to arouse strong compassion, imagine that your mother is undergoing intense suffering, that she lacks everything she needs, that she is dying of hunger and thirst and is being treated badly. Imagine other painful situations she is facing. You can do this for any person you have chosen as the object of your meditation. It could be a child, a loyal friend or an animal that you love. You could also imagine, for example, a doe pursued by hunters and their pack of dogs. Cornered and filled with panic, she jumps off a cliff and breaks her bones. The hunters find her dying and finish her off with their knives.

Picture all kinds of suffering in your mind with graphic precision. Imagine old or sick people suffering from the agonies of disease, poor people who barely have enough to live on. Think of those who have been deprived of everything they need and also of people who are victims of their own minds and are being driven mad by desire or hatred.

Do not forget to include in your love and compassion all those people you consider to be your enemies and who cause you trouble. Visualize in front of you all humanity gathered into an immense crowd and recall that, like you, they have suffered in many ways through an infinite cycle of lifetimes.

When an intense feeling of compassion arises, begin the practice of exchange. Think that as you breathe out, along with your breath you send out to those who are suffering all your happiness, your vitality, your good fortune, your health and so on, in the form of refreshing and radiant white nectar. Imagine that you give them these benefits without any reserve and that this nectar fulfils all their needs. If their life is in danger, imagine it is prolonged; if they are poor, imagine they receive whatever they need; if they are sick, imagine they are healed; and if they are miserable, imagine they find happiness.

As you breathe in, imagine you are taking upon yourself, in the form of a dark mass, all the illness, physical and mental problems, as well as the emotional disturbances of these beings, and that this exchange relieves their torments. Imagine their suffering comes back to you like a mist blown by the wind. When you have absorbed, transformed and eliminated all their pain and trouble, feel a great joy, mixed with a feeling of non-attachment.

Repeat this practice many times until it becomes second nature. Never think you have done enough for those who are suffering.

This method can be applied at any time in any circumstances, and in particular when you yourself are suffering. In this case, generating altruism and compassion opens your heart to other people instead of letting your pain push you deeper into self-centred distress. As a bonus it also acts like a soothing balm on your own pain. You can do this exercise at any time, in and out of meditation sessions, and apply it to all activities of your daily life.

Variation One

As you breathe out, think that your heart is a brilliant shining sphere, from which rays of white light stream out, bringing happiness to all beings in all directions.

As you breathe in, take in the torments of all beings in the form of a dense dark cloud that penetrates into your heart and dissolves into a mass of white light without leaving a trace.

Variation Two

Imagine your body multiplies itself into an infinite number of forms that reach the far ends of the universe, taking on all the suffering of all beings they encounter and offering them their happiness. Then your body transforms into clothing for those who are cold, into food for those who are hungry and into a refuge for those who are shelterless. Then you become a 'wish-fulfilling gem' somewhat larger than your body and sparkling like a magnificent blue sapphire that naturally satisfies all the needs of anyone.

This practice allows you to associate your breathing with the development of compassion. It is very simple and can be used at any moment in your daily life — when you are sitting on a train, waiting in line or in a traffic jam, or just when you are enjoying a respite from your everyday activities.

Soothing Physical Pain

Physical pain is an experience we all have to face. But the subjective reaction we have to it varies significantly from person to person. The sensation of pain, for example, can be considerably amplified by anticipating it and by an anxious urge to suppress it. At such a moment the mildest of pains can become intolerable. Chronic pain can be made much more tolerable by changing our attitude towards it and imbuing it with some meaning.

Studies in neuroscience have shown that the way we evaluate pain can be modulated by our anticipation of it and depends to a great extent on the way our mind deals with it. We have more tolerance for pains that have a predictable duration and intensity. Predictability helps us to be ready for them when they arise. Thus we can manage them better than pains whose intensity is subject to increase and whose duration is unknown. If pain gets completely out of our control and we think it might last indefinitely, then our mind might easily be completely overwhelmed by suffering.

Another point is that giving pain a meaning helps us to bear it. We accept the painful secondary effects of a medical treatment we hope will cure us. We might also be willing to experience pain for the sake of helping another person. This is the case when a parent or friend gives blood or donates an organ to save the life of a dear one. The same goes for the pain, sometimes quite intense, that athletes endure in their training. They fully accept that pain because it results in improving their performance. Some athletes say that the more intense the pain is, the more they appreciate it as feedback on the intensity of their training. These same athletes report that they are much more negatively affected by unforeseen pain that has no value for them: for example, an injury that occurs in the course of their training. Giving pain a meaning gives us power over it and does away with the anxiety that comes with feelings of confusion and helplessness. By contrast, if we react with fear, resentment, discouragement, lack of understanding or a feeling of helplessness, then instead of just experiencing one pain, we add several more to it.

The most difficult cases are those of chronic, intense and persistent pain that overpowers our other sensations. Such pain dominates the mind and our relation to the world; it accompanies our every thought and deed. I once heard a sick person say: 'Intense chronic pain is like a stone thrown into a pond: its waves spread throughout your life. There's no place to run from it.' All the same, we can suffer intense pain without letting it destroy our positive vision of life. If we are able to attain a certain level of inner peace, it is easier to maintain our strength of mind or to regain it quickly even when we are confronted by difficult circumstances.

People who have lived through an accident, torture or other kinds of intense pain have indicated that later on they felt 'more human' than before. They felt a deeper appreciation of the world around them, of the beauty of nature, and of the good qualities of the people they met. They said they, 'considered every moment of their lives a priceless treasure.'[29]

So how can we manage our pain rather than being the victim of it? If you cannot escape it, it is better to make use of it than try to resist it. Whether you fall into the deepest of depressions or maintain your strength of mind and your will to live, either way the pain will be there. In the second case, you will be able to preserve your dignity and self-confidence. And that makes a big difference.

Buddhism teaches different methods for achieving this. I will explain four of them. The first consists simply in mindfully observing the pain without interpreting it. The second makes use of mental imagery. The third allows us to transform the pain by awakening love and compassion. The last involves examining the nature of the suffering, and, by extension, the nature of the suffering mind.

Meditation One: Mindfulness

As explained in the texts below, observe with pure mindfulness the sensation of pain without interpreting, rejecting or fearing it. Immerse yourself in the mindfulness of the present moment. Your sensation will then retain its intensity but lose its repellent character.

Sources of Inspiration

Most of us regard pain as a threat to our physical well-being. On one hand, when we worry or allow ourselves to become preoccupied by this threat, the pain itself almost always increases. On the other hand, if we consider pain or discomfort as an object of meditation, we can use such sensations to increase our capacity for clarity.

—*Yongey Mingyur Rinpoche*[30]

[How does one work with pain as an object of meditation?] A pure unobstructed awareness of the pain will experience it simply as a flowing pattern of energy and nothing more. No thought and no rejection. Just energy... But the human mind conceptualises such occurrences as 'the pain'. This is a concept. It is a label, something added to the sensation itself. You find yourself building a mental image... You will probably find yourself thinking [something like], 'I have a pain in my leg.' 'I' is a concept. It is something extra added to the pain experience. When you introduce the 'I' into the process, you are building a conceptual gap between the reality and the awareness that is viewing that reality. Thoughts such as 'me', 'my', or 'mine' have no place in direct awareness. They are extraneous addenda, and insidious ones at that. When you bring 'me' into the picture, you are identifying with the pain. That simply adds emphasis to it. If you leave the 'I' out of the operation, pain is not painful. It is just a pure surging energy flow.

— *Bhante Henepola Gunaratna*[31]

Meditation Two: The Power of Mental Imagery
Visualize a soothing, warm and luminous nectar penetrates the place where the pain is at its worst, dissolves it little by little and finally transforms it into a sensation of well-being. This nectar fills your entire body, and the painful sensation fades away. If the pain increases in intensity, then increase the strength of the nectar accordingly, thinking that each atom of pain is now replaced by an atom of well-being. In this way, transmute the very essence of the pain into bliss.

Meditation Three: The Force of Compassion

Arouse a powerful feeling of altruistic love and compassion towards all beings, and think: 'I wish so much to put an end to my suffering. But others beside me are tormented by pain comparable to my own, and sometimes even worse. How I wish that they too could be liberated from that pain.' You may also imagine that you have deliberately volunteered to experience that pain to spare someone, your child for instance, from enduring it. Then your pain will no longer be experienced as something degrading or overwhelming. Filled now with altruism, you stop asking yourself bitterly, 'Why me?' but rejoice that someone else has been spared that suffering.

When you are totally absorbed in yourself, you are vulnerable and an easy prey to confusion and feelings of distress, helplessness and anxiety. If, instead of that, you feel a strong sense of empathy, combined with unconditional love, towards the suffering of others, resignation will be replaced by courage, depression by love and meanness by openness towards people around you.

Meditation Four: Contemplating the Nature of the Mind Itself

Contemplate the nature of pain. Even if it is sharp and penetrating, ask yourself what colour is it, what shape is it, what other unchangeable characteristics it might have. With this kind of enquiry, the characteristics of the pain get blurry the minute you try to focus on it. You will soon recognize that behind the pain there is a pure awareness, the very same one that is at the source of any other sensation or thought. Relax your mind and try to let the pain rest within this pure awareness, free from any mental constructs. By taking this approach you are no longer just the passive victim of the pain and, little by little, you will be able to face it and overcome the bruising negative effects it has on your mind.

This last approach is certainly not easy, but experience shows that it is possible. I have known a number of meditators who have applied this method in the course of particularly painful terminal illnesses. They seemed remarkably calm and relatively little affected by the pain.

Francisco Varela, a dear friend and well-known researcher in the cognitive sciences who had practised Buddhist meditation for years, told me a few weeks before his death from an extensively metastasised cancer that he was able to remain almost constantly within a pure state of awareness. Then his physical pain seemed remote and did not get in the way of his inner peace. He needed only weak doses of painkillers and was able to maintain his lucidity and serenity until his last breath.

Deep Insight
(*Vipashyana*)

Now let's explore another meditation practice, deep insight (*vipashyana* in Sanskrit, *vipassana* in Pali). The way we perceive others and the world in general considerably influences our behaviour and the way we live. We constantly impose our narrow view of reality on the world, and the resulting distortions turn into causes of frustration and suffering, because they inevitably clash with reality. How often have we decided that somebody or something was totally desirable or detestable? Taken in by the solidity of these concepts, we cling to 'me' and 'mine' with tremendous tenacity.

Imagine you perceive the world of phenomena as a dynamic flow of interdependent events of which the ceaselessly changing characteristics are the results of causes and conditions and not intrinsic qualities of the objects they appear to define. The concepts of me and mine will now appear to you much more fluid and will no longer be the object of such powerful fixations.

Cultivating deep insight in this way is an essential practice for rooting out suffering and the fundamental misunderstandings that are the source of it.

To develop deep insight, it is absolutely necessary to have a clear, concentrated and stable mind, which is why it is important to prepare by practising inner calm or *shamatha*. *Shamatha* makes it possible to calm afflictive emotions temporarily, but it is not enough by itself because it cannot eradicate them completely. Therefore we need to continue by practising deep insight. This will help us to recognize the basic nature of consciousness, the way emotions arise and become entangled with each other, and how our mental fabrications reinforce the self-centredness of the ego. Deep insight will allow us, first through analysis and then through direct experience, to understand that phenomena are impermanent and interdependent and thus do not have the tangible, independent existence that is ordinarily attributed to them. The result of this will be greater truth and freedom in the way we perceive the world. We will no longer be prisoners of our self-centred vision. We will be better able to cope with the emotional reactions brought about by our inter-action with our surroundings.

Vipashyana can be practised at different levels and in different ways. I will examine some aspects of it here:

* How to arrive at a more accurate understanding of reality.
* How to free ourselves from the torments of afflictive emotions.
* How to unmask the deceptions of the ego and the consequences of grasping on to the notion of an independent self, and understand their influence on our suffering and well-being.
* How to understand the fundamental nature of the mind.

Understanding Reality Better

What do I mean by reality? According to Buddhism, reality means the real nature of things, unmodified by the mental fabrications that create a discrepancy between the way things appear to us and the way they really are. This discrepancy is the source of continual conflicts with our world. Usually we perceive the external world as a composite of independent entities to which we attribute characteristics that seem to be an inherent part of them. Thus things appear to us as intrinsically 'nice' or 'not nice' and people as basically 'good' or 'bad'. The 'I,' or the ego, that perceives all this also seems real and concrete to us. This misunderstanding, which Buddhism refers to as 'ignorance', brings about the powerful reflexes of attachment and aversion, which in turn lead to an endless succession of painful experiences.

According to Buddhist analysis, the world is a result of the coming together of an infinite number of causes and conditions that are continually changing. Just as a rainbow is formed at the precise moment the sun shines on a collection of raindrops and disappears as soon as the factors that produce it are no longer present, phenomena exist in an essentially interdependent mode and have no independent and permanent existence. Ultimate reality is therefore described as empty of independently existing animate or inanimate phenomena. Everything is relationship; nothing exists in and of itself. Once this essential idea has been understood and assimilated, our erroneous perception of our ego and our world gives way to an accurate view of the nature of things and beings — wisdom. Wisdom is not a simple intellectual construction or a compilation of information. It arises from a precise methodology that allows us progressively to eliminate mental blindness and the afflictive emotions that derive from it and, in that way, free us from the principal cause of suffering.

The goal of the following meditation is to transform our perception of reality. It is described in contemporary terms, but it is based on a classical Buddhist philosophical analysis that can be found in the reference works cited in the bibliography.

Meditation

Imagine a freshly bloomed rose. It is so beautiful! Now imagine that you are a small insect nibbling on one of its petals. It tastes so good! Now imagine yourself as a tiger standing before this rose. For him, it makes no difference whether it is a flower or a bale of hay. Now transport yourself into the heart of this rose and imagine yourself as an atom there. You no longer exist except as pathways of energy in a kaleidoscopic universe, amid a whorl of particles passing through nearly empty space. Where did the rose go? Where is its colour, form, texture, fragrance, its taste, its beauty? As for the particles, if you look at them closely, are they solid objects? Not really, the physicists say. They are events arising in the quantum void; they are 'waves of probability' and, ultimately, of energy. Energy? Is that an entity? Isn't it more like a potential for manifestation that neither exists nor doesn't exist? What is left of the rose?

Sources of Inspiration

Like a flickering star, a mirage or a flame,
Like a magical illusion, a dewdrop, or a bubble on
  a stream,
Like a dream, a flash of lightning, or a cloud
See all compounded things as being like these.

—*Chandrakirti*

Like reflections on the surface of a clear lake,
The multitude of phenomena manifests,
Completely devoid of inherent existence.
This very day, acquire the certitude
That everything is no more than reflections
  of emptiness.

—*Longchen Rabjam*[32]

Subject and object are like sandalwood and its fragrance. Samsara and nirvana are like ice and water. Appearances and emptiness are like clouds and the sky. Thoughts and the nature of the mind are like waves and the ocean.

—*Geshe Chayulpa*[33]

Lakes and rivers can freeze in winter and the water can become so solid that people, animals and carts travel back and forth on its surface. At the approach of spring, the earth warms up and the waters thaw. What remains then of all that solid ice? Water is soft and fluid, ice hard and sharp. We cannot say that they are identical, but neither are they different

– ice is only frozen water, and water is only melted ice.

It is the same with our perceptions of the external world. To be attached to the reality of phenomena, tormented by attraction and repulsion, and obsessed by the eight worldly preoccupations[34] is what causes the mind to freeze. Melt the ice of your concepts so that the fluid water of free perception can flow.

—Dilgo Khyentse Rinpoche[35]

Recognition of the nature of the mind and an accurate understanding of the phenomenal world are essential for our quest for happiness. If the mind relies on totally erroneous views about the nature of things and maintains them, it will be very difficult for us to transform ourselves and achieve freedom. Developing a correct view is not a question of faith or adherence to dogma but of clear understanding. This arises from a correct analysis of reality. Through this, little by little, the belief in the inherent existence of things, in which our erroneous conception of the world is rooted, is cast into doubt and replaced by an accurate view of phenomena.

— 14th Dalai Lama[36]

Dealing with Thoughts and Emotions

We often hear that the aim of Buddhism in general and meditation in particular is to suppress the emotions. Whether this is true or not depends on what we mean by emotion. If we are talking about mental disturbances such as hatred and jealousy, why not get rid of them? If we are talking about powerful altruistic love or about compassion for suffering beings, why not develop these qualities? These are the goals of meditation.

Meditation teaches us how to deal with bursts of malicious anger or jealousy, with waves of uncontrolled desire and with irrational fears. It frees us from the tyranny of mental states that obscure our judgement and are the source of constant distress. Buddhism speaks of mental poisons, because these mental states truly poison our existence and that of others.

The word 'emotion' comes from the Latin *emovere*,

which means 'to set in motion'. An emotion is thus what sets the mind in motion, whether that motion takes the form of harmful, neutral or wholesome thoughts. Emotion conditions the mind and leads it to adopt a certain perspective, a certain view of things. This view can be in accord with reality, as in the case of altruistic love and compassion, or distorted, as in the case of hatred or craving. As I pointed out earlier, altruistic love is an awareness of the fact that all beings wish, as we do, to be free from suffering. It is based on recognition of the basic interdependence of all beings, which we all are a part of. By contrast, hatred distorts reality by exaggerating the faults of its object and ignoring that object's good qualities. In the same way, avid desire makes us perceive its object as desirable from every point of view and ignore its faults.

So we cannot but agree that certain emotions are afflictive and others are beneficial. If an emotion strengthens our inner peace and encourages us to seek the welfare of others, we can consider it positive or constructive. If it destroys our serenity, deeply troubles our mind and leads us to harm others, it is negative or destructive. That is what differentiates, for instance, strong indignation or 'holy anger' with regard to an injustice from anger motivated by the intention to harm somebody.

The important thing, therefore, is not to try to suppress our emotions, which would be futile anyway, but to work with them in such a way that they contribute to our inner peace and lead us to think, speak and act in a way that is helpful to others. To that end, we have to avoid becoming the helpless toy of our emotions. Learn to dissolve the negative emotions as they arise and cultivate the positive ones.

We should also understand that it is the accumulation and interlocking of fleeting emotions and thoughts that create our moods. These moods can last for a few hours or a few days, and over the long term form our character tendencies and traits. That is why, if we learn to deal with our thoughts and emotions in a good way – little by little, thought after thought, emotion by emotion, day after day – in the end we will be able to transform our way of being. This is the essence of mind-training and meditation with regard to emotions.

Of the various methods for dealing with afflictive emotions through meditation, we will explain two. The first consists of applying antidotes. The second is not identifying with these temporary disturbances while at the same time recognizing their true nature.

APPLYING ANTIDOTES

The word antidote here refers to a state of mind that is diametrically opposed to the afflictive emotion we want to overcome. In the same way as a glass of water cannot be hot and cold at the same time, we cannot wish simultaneously to benefit and harm the same person. What we have to do is cultivate remedies powerful enough to neutralize the negative emotions that afflict us.

Seen from another point of view, the more kindness and benevolence we develop, the less room there will be in our mind for their opposites malice and ill will. The more light there is in a room, the more darkness is dispelled. In the meditations that follow take desire and then malicious anger as examples.

DESIRE: Everyone would agree that desire is natural and plays an essential role in helping us to realize our aspirations. But desire is only a blind force that in itself is neither helpful nor harmful. Everything depends on what kind of influence it has over us. It is capable both of providing inspiration in our lives and poisoning them. It can encourage us to act in a way that is constructive for ourselves and others, but it can also bring about intense pain. The latter is what happens when it becomes a possessive and pervasive craving. It then forces us to become dependent on the very causes of suffering. In that case it is a source of unhappiness, and there is no advantage in continuing to be ruled by it. Apply the antidote of inner freedom to the desire that causes suffering.

Meditation

If you are the victim of a strong desire that is troubling you and won't leave you alone, begin by examining its main characteristics and identifying the appropriate antidotes.

One aspect of desire is urgency. To counter that urgency, calm your thoughts and observe the coming and going of the breath as described earlier.

Desire also has a restrictive and disturbing aspect. As an antidote to this, imagine the comforting and soothing quality of inner freedom. Spend a few moments allowing a feeling of freedom to arise and grow.

Desire tends to distort reality and to make you view its object as fundamentally desirable.

In order to regain a more accurate view of things, take the time to examine all aspects of the object of your desire and meditate for a few moments on its less attractive and less desirable sides.

Finally, let your mind relax into the peace of awareness, free from hope and fear, and appreciate the freshness of the present moment, which acts like a balm on the burning of desire.

Sources of Inspiration

A peaceful mind does not mean a mind empty of thoughts, sensations, and emotions. A peaceful mind is not an absent one.

—*Thich Nhat Hanh*[37]

Handle desire in the following manner. Notice the thought or sensation when it arises. Notice the mental state of desire which accompanies it as a separate thing. Notice the exact extent or degree of this desire. Then notice how long it lasts and when it finally disappears. When you have done that, return your attention to breathing.

—*Bhante Henepola Gunaratna*[38]

If bliss it is to scratch an itch
What greater bliss no itch at all?
So too, the worldly, desirous, find some bliss,
But greatest is the bliss with no desire.

—*Nagarjuna*[39]

ANGER: The impulse of self-centred anger, which is the precursor of hatred, is to push aside whoever stands in the way of the ego's demands. It has no consideration for the welfare of others. It expresses itself as open hostility when the ego is in attack mode and as resentment and bitterness when the ego is wounded, scorned or slighted. Basic anger can also be associated with malice, the conscious desire to hurt someone.

The mind overrun by animosity and resentment shuts

itself up in illusion and convinces itself that the source of its frustration lies entirely outside itself. The truth is that even if resentment is triggered by an external object, it is not located anywhere else but in our mind. Moreover, if our hatred is a response to somebody else's hatred, we have stepped into a vicious circle that has no end. The following meditation is not intended to suppress hatred but to turn our mind towards that which is diametrically opposed to it – love and compassion.

Meditation

Think of someone who has been malicious towards you or people close to you, someone who has made you suffer. Also, think of people that are causing, or have caused, tremendous suffering to others. Realize that if the mental poisons that led them to behave this way were to vanish from their minds, they would naturally cease to be your enemies and those of humanity. Wish with all your heart for this transformation to take place.

To do this, make use of the meditation on altruistic love in which, as you saw above, you formulate this wish as follows: 'May all sentient beings be liberated from suffering and the causes of suffering. May hatred, greed, arrogance, contempt, indifference, miserliness and jealousy vanish from their minds and be replaced by altruistic love, contentment, modesty, appreciation, concern, generosity and sympathy.' Let this feeling of unconditional benevolence pervade all your thoughts.

Sources of Inspiration

It is the only thing we can do... Each of us must turn inward and destroy in himself all that he thinks he ought to destroy in others. And remember that every atom of hate we add to this world makes it still more inhospitable.

—*Etty Hillesum*[40]

I no longer believe that we can change anything in the world until we have first changed ourselves. And that seems to me the only less to be learned from this war.

—*Etty Hillesum*[41]

It is time to redirect hatred away from its usual targets, your so-called enemies, and towards itself. Indeed, hatred is your real enemy and it is hatred that you should destroy.

—*Dilgo Khyentse Rinpoche*

By giving in to anger, we are not necessarily harming our enemy but we are definitely harming ourselves. We lose our sense of inner peace, we do everything wrong, our digestion is bad, we cannot sleep well, we put off our guests or we cast furious glances at those who have the impudence of being in our way. If we have a pet, we forget to feed it. We make life impossible for those who live with us, and even our dearest friends are kept at a distance. Since there are fewer and fewer people who sympathize with us, we feel more and more lonely... To what end? Even if we allow our rage to go all the way, we will never eliminate all our enemies. Do you know of anyone who ever has? As long as we harbour that inner enemy of anger or hatred, however successful we are at destroying our outer enemies today, others will emerge tomorrow.

—*14th Dalai Lama*[42]

STOP IDENTIFYING WITH EMOTIONS

The second way to deal with afflictive emotions is to dissociate ourselves mentally from the emotion that is troubling us. Usually we identify with our emotions completely. When we are overcome by anxiety or by a fit of anger, we are at one with it. It is omnipresent in our mind, leaving no room for other mental states such as inner peace, patience or for considering reasoning that might calm our displeasure. However, if at that moment we are still capable of a little presence of mind – a capability that we can be trained to develop – we can stop identifying with our anger.

The mind is, in fact, capable of examining what is happening within it. All we need to do is observe our emotions in the same way we would observe an external event taking place in front of us. The part of our mind that is conscious of the anger is just simply conscious – it is not angry. In other words, mindfulness is not affected by the emotion it is observing. Understanding that makes it possible to step back, to realize that this emotion has no substance and to leave enough space for it to dissolve by itself.

By doing so, we avoid two extremes, each as bad as the other: repressing our emotion, which would then remain in a dark corner of our consciousness like a time bomb; or letting the emotion explode at the expense of those around us and of our own inner peace. Not identifying with emotions is a fundamental antidote that is applicable to all kinds of emotions, in any circumstances.

In the following meditations, I make use of the examples of anger and anxiety, but the process described would be the same for any other afflictive emotion.

Meditation One

Imagine that you are overcome by very strong anger. It seems to you that you have no choice but to let yourself be carried away. Helpless, your mind is repeatedly drawn to the object that triggered your rage as iron is drawn to a magnet. Someone has insulted you, and the image of this person and his words constantly come to your mind. Every time you think of them, you set loose a new flood of resentment, which nourishes the vicious cycle of thoughts and reactions to those thoughts.

It is time to change your tactics. Turn away from the object of your anger and contemplate the anger itself. This is a little like watching a fire, but no longer feeding it with wood. No matter how intense the fire is, in a little time it will go out all by itself. In the same way, if you turn your attention to simply looking at the anger, it is impossible for it to persist on its own. No matter how intense an emotion is, it will wear itself out and disappear naturally once you stop feeding it.

Also understand that in the end the most powerful anger attack is no more than a thought. Take a closer look at this. Where does the anger get the power to dominate you to this degree? Does it have a weapon? Can it burn you like fire? Can it crush you like a rock? Can you locate it in your chest, in your heart, or in your head? If the answer to this last question seems to be yes, does it have a colour or a form? You would really have great difficulty in attributing such characteristics to it. When you look at a big black cloud in a stormy sky, it appears to be substantial enough to sit on, but if you fly into this cloud, you will find there is nothing solid to hold on to. There is nothing there but intangible mist. Similarly, when you attentively examine anger, you will find nothing in it that could justify the tyrannical influence it has over you. The more you try to pin it down, the more it melts away under your gaze like frost under the rays of the rising sun.

Finally, where does this anger come from? Where is it right now? Where does it disappear to? All you can say is that it comes from your mind, endures there for a while, then fades away back into it. As for the mind itself, it is ungraspable. It is not a distinct entity; it is nothing more than a stream of experiences.

Meditation Two

If you notice that you have become anxious — when you are about to miss a plane, for instance — try to simply be fully aware of your anxiety. As you continue to do this, you will soon notice your anxiety begins to be less oppressive and then gradually fades away. Why? Before you apply mindfulness, anxiety is the main component of your mind, filling its entire landscape. As you become aware of it, you experience both anxiety and the awareness of it. The part of your mind that is aware of anxiety is not anxious, it is just aware. Anxiety is now just one aspect of your mental landscape. As your awareness becomes more and more pervasive, anxiety loses its intensity and its grip on your mind. Eventually it vanishes.

If every time a powerful emotion arises, you learn to deal with it intelligently, not only will you master the art of liberating emotions at the moment they appear, but you will also erode the very tendencies that cause the emotions to arise. In this way, your character traits and your way of being will gradually be transformed.

This method might seem difficult at the beginning, especially in the heat of the moment, but with practice, you will gradually get used to it. When anger or any other afflictive emotion begins to hatch in your mind, you will be able to identify it on the spot and be able to deal with it before it gets out of hand. It's a little like knowing the identity of a pickpocket: even if he mingles with the crowd, you can spot him immediately and keep your eye on him so that he won't be able to steal your wallet.

Thus, by becoming more and more familiar with the mechanisms of the mind and by cultivating mindfulness, you will reach the point where you no longer let sparks of nascent emotions turn into forest fires that can destroy your own happiness and that of others.

This method can be used with all the afflictive emotions. It enables you to make a connection between the practice of meditation and the concerns of everyday life. If you get into the habit of looking at thoughts the moment they arise and letting them dissipate before they take hold of you, it will be much easier to retain mastery of your mind and to deal with the conflicting emotions in the thick of everyday activities.

Sources of Inspiration

Remember that thoughts are only the product of the momentary confluence of a great number of factors. In themselves they do not exist. Thus, the moment they arise, recognize that their nature is emptiness. They will immediately lose their power to produce other thoughts, and the chain of illusion will be broken. Recognize the emptiness of thoughts and let them relax into the natural clarity of the transparent and unaltered mind.

—Dilgo Khyentse Rinpoche[43]

When sunlight falls on a crystal, lights of all colours of the rainbow appear; yet they have no substance that you can grasp. Likewise, all thoughts in their infinite variety — devotion, compassion, harmfulness, desire — are utterly without substance. This is the mind of the Buddha. There is no thought that is something other than emptiness; if you recognize the void nature of thoughts at the very moment they arise, they will dissolve. Attachment and hatred will never be able to disturb the mind. Deluded emotions will collapse by themselves. No negative actions will be accumulated, so no suffering will follow.

—*Dilgo Khyentse Rinpoche*[44]

Trying to Find the Ego

The idea of getting away from the influence of ego might be puzzling, especially if we think that in doing so we are tampering with our basic identity. Understanding the nature of the ego and the way it functions is crucial if we want to liberate ourselves from suffering. We know that at every moment, from the time of our birth onward, our body has been continually changing and innumerable new experiences have taken place in our mind. Still we instinctively imagine that somewhere deep down within us, there resides an enduring entity that endows our personality with solid reality and permanence. This intuition may seem so evident we don't think it is necessary to examine it any further. We end up developing a powerful attachment to the notions of 'me' and 'mine' — *my* body, *my* name, *my* mind, *my* possessions, *my* friends and so on. This attachment brings with it either a desire to possess or repulse the other. An insurmountable duality between self and other becomes crystallized in our mind. Our being becomes equated with an imaginary entity: the self. From this mental construction arises an exaggerated sense of the importance of this self. The ego places its fictitious identity at the centre of all our experiences.

However, as soon as we seriously analyse the nature of the ego, we see that it is impossible to pinpoint a distinct identity that corresponds to it. In the end, we realize the ego is no more than a concept that we associate with the continuum of experiences that is our consciousness.

Our identification with the ego is fundamentally dysfunctional, because it is out of step with reality. We attribute to the ego the qualities of permanence, singularity and autonomy. The ego fragments the world and definitively solidifies the division between self and other, mine and not-mine. Because it is based on a mistake, it is constantly threatened by reality, and this gives us a deep and ongoing sense of insecurity. Since we are aware of the ego's vulnerability, we try by all means available to protect and reinforce it. As a result we feel aversion towards anything that threatens it and attraction towards anything that feeds it. From these impulses of repulsion and attraction, a multitude of conflicting emotions is born.

We might think that by devoting most of our time to satisfying and reinforcing the ego, we are adopting the best possible strategy for achieving happiness. But this turns out to be a losing bet, because just the opposite happens. By imagining an independent ego, we put ourselves in a state of conflict with the nature of things, and this results in endless frustration and pain. Devoting all our energy to this imaginary entity critically damages the quality of our lives.

The only kind of self-confidence the ego can achieve is an artificial one, based on shaky factors, such as power, success, beauty, physical strength, intellectual brilliance and the opinions of others — all things that are related to our image. Genuine self-confidence is something entirely different. Paradoxically, it is a natural quality of the absence of ego. To dispel the illusion of the ego is to free yourself from a fundamental weakness. Self-confidence based on non-ego brings a sense of freedom that is not subject to emotional contingencies. You experience a lack of vulnerability to the judgements of others and an inner acceptance of whatever circumstances may exist. This sense of freedom manifests as openness towards whatever arises. It is not something frigid and aloof; it is not the dry detachment or indifference people sometimes imagine when they think of Buddhist non-attachment. Rather it is a daring and kind-hearted availability that reaches out to all beings.

When the ego is not revelling in its triumphs, it nourishes itself on its failures by setting itself up as a victim. Fed by its ceaseless broodings, its suffering confirms its existence just as much as its euphoria does. Whether it is riding high or feeling reduced, slighted and ignored, the ego solidifies itself by paying attention only to itself. 'The ego is the result of a mental activity that creates and keeps an imaginary entity alive in our mind.'[45] It is an impostor who gets caught up in his own game. One of the functions of deep insight, *vipashyana*, is to unmask the deception of the ego.

The fact is that we are not this ego, we are not this anger, we are not this despair. Our most fundamental level of experience is pure awareness, the primary quality of consciousness that I referred to earlier that is the basis of all experience, of all emotion, of all reasoning, of all concept, of all mental constructs, *including the ego*. But attention, which is pure consciousness, pure awareness, is not some new entity more subtle than the ego; rather it is the fundamental quality of our mental stream.

The ego is nothing more than a mental construct that lasts longer than the others because it is constantly being reinforced by our mental associations. But that does not prevent it from being an illusory concept that is devoid of all inherent existence. A movie that lasts one hundred years is no more real than a movie that lasts an hour. This stubborn label that is the ego can only stick to the stream of our consciousness through the application of the magic glue of mental confusion.

In order to unmask the deception of the ego, we must carry out a full and thorough investigation. If we sense the presence of a thief in our house, we have to look through every room, every nook and cranny, every possible hiding place, until we reach the point where we are sure there is really no one there. Only then can our minds rest.

Meditation

Look and see what it is that composes the 'I', the ego. Is it the body? The body is a composite of flesh and bone. Is it consciousness? Consciousness is a succession of fleeting thoughts. Your history? Your history is only memories of things that no longer exist. Your name? You attach all sorts of concepts to a name – your genealogy, your reputation, your social status – but in the end it is no more than a combination of letters.

If the ego really was your profound essence, your fear of doing away with it would be understandable. However, if it is only an illusion, liberating yourself from it would not be destroying the core of your being, but just correcting an error and opening your eyes to reality. Error offers no more resistance to knowledge than darkness does to light. Darkness that has lasted for millions of years can disappear in an instant the moment a lamp is lit.

When the 'I' ceases to be considered the centre of the world, you naturally develop concern for others. Self-centred contemplation of your own suffering discourages you, whereas altruistic care for the suffering of others just redoubles your determination to work for their relief. So the profound sense of an 'I' at the core of your being is clearly something you have to subject to an honest examination.

Where is this 'I' located? It can't be in my body, because when I say, 'I'm sad,' it's my consciousness that feels the sense of sadness, not my body. Is the 'I', then, only in my consciousness? That is far from being clear. When I say, 'Somebody pushed me,' is it my consciousness that was pushed? Obviously not. But the 'I' cannot be located outside both the body and the consciousness. So is the notion of 'I' to be connected with a combination of body and consciousness? That would take us to a very abstract concept.

The only solution to this dilemma is to consider the 'I' as a mental designation for a dynamic process, a composite of changing relationships that bring together your sensations, your mental images, your emotions and your concepts. In the end, the 'I' is no more than a name you use to designate a continuum in the same way that you call a river Amazon or Ganges. Every river has a history. It flows through a unique landscape and its water might have healing properties or be polluted. For that reason, it is legitimate to give it a name and distinguish it from another river. However, no entity exists in the river that could be called its core or essence. In the same way, the 'I', or the ego, exists only as a convention, not at all in the form of an entity that constitutes the core of your being.

The ego always has something to lose and something to gain. Natural simplicity of mind has nothing to lose and nothing to gain. It is not necessary to add anything to it or take anything away. The ego feeds on dwelling on the past and anticipating the future, but it cannot survive in the simplicity of the present moment. Rest in that simplicity, in the mindfulness of the present moment, which is freedom, the ultimate resolution of all conflicts, all fabrications, all mental projections, all distortions, all identifications and all divisions.

*

It is worthwhile to devote a little of our time to letting our mind rest in the inner calm that will help you to better understand the role of the ego in our life. This can be done both through analysis and direct experience. As long as a sense of self-importance rules our being, we will never know lasting peace. The very cause of pain itself will remain hidden deep within and will deprive us of the most essential of all freedoms.

Abandoning grasping on to the ego and ceasing to identify with it brings tremendous inner freedom. This is a freedom that allows us to relate to anyone we meet in any situation with naturalness, goodwill, courage and serenity. Having nothing to gain and nothing to lose, we are free to give and receive everything.

Meditating on the Nature of the Mind

Having a clear understanding of the mind is essential to unravel the mechanisms of happiness and suffering. That is why psychologists, specialists in neuroscience and philosophers investigate the nature of the mind. It is, after all, our mind that we have to deal with from morning till night; and it is our mind, in the end, that determines the quality of every moment of our existence. So if knowing the mind's true nature and understanding its mechanisms will exercise a decisive influence on our quality of life, then we have good reason to investigate it. If we do not investigate it, if we fail to understand our own mind, then we remain a stranger to ourselves.

When the mind examines itself, what can it learn about its own nature? The first thing it notices is the endless series of thoughts that pass through it. These feed our sensations, our imagination, our memories and our projections about the future. Do we also find a 'luminous' quality in the mind that illuminates our experience, no matter what its content? This luminous quality is the fundamental cognitive faculty that underlies all thought. It is that which, when we are angry, sees the anger without letting itself be drawn into it. This simple, pure awareness can be called pure consciousness, because it can be perceived even in the absence of concepts and mental constructs.

The practice of meditation reveals that when we let our thoughts calm down, we are able to remain for a few moments in the non-conceptual experience of pure awareness. It is this fundamental aspect of consciousness, free from the veils of confusion, that Buddhism calls 'the nature of mind'.

Thoughts arise out of pure awareness and dissolve back into it just as waves arise in the ocean and fall back into it without ever becoming anything other than the ocean itself. It is essential to realize this if we want to free ourselves from the habitual, automatic patterns of thought that create suffering. Identifying the fundamental nature of mind and knowing how to rest in it in a non-dual and non-conceptual way is one of the essential conditions for inner peace and liberation from suffering.

Meditation

A thought arises as though from nowhere. It might be a pleasant thought or a troubling one. It stays for a few moments and then dies away, to be replaced by others. When it disappears, like the sound of a bell fading, where does it go? No one can say. Certain thoughts recur frequently in your mind where they create states ranging from joy to sadness, desire to indifference, resentment to sympathy. In this way, thoughts have tremendous power to condition our state of being. But where do they get this power? They don't have an army at their command, nor do they possess fuel to start a fire with; they don't have stones they can stone you with. They are only mental constructs, so they should not be able to harm you.

Let your mind observe itself. Thoughts arise.

The mind exists in some way, because you experience it. Apart from that, what could be said about it? Examine your mind and the thoughts that arise there. Can any concrete characteristics be attributed to them? Do they have a location? Do they have a colour? A form? The more you look, the less you find. You note of course that the mind has a capacity to know, but it has no other intrinsic and real characteristic. This is the reason Buddhism defines the mind as a continuum of experiences. It does not constitute a distinct entity, it is 'empty of inherent existence'. Having found nothing in any way substantial, remain for a few moments in this state of not having found anything.

When a thought appears, just let it arise and pass away by itself, without either blocking or prolonging it. During the brief time that your mind is not burdened by any discursive thought, contemplate its nature. In this gap, after past thoughts have ceased and future thoughts have not yet appeared, do you perceive a consciousness that is pure and luminous? Remain a few moments in this state of natural simplicity, free from concepts.

As we gradually familiarize ourselves with the nature of mind and learn to let thoughts pass away as soon as they arise — just like a letter written on water — we begin to progress more easily on the path of inner freedom. Automatic thought patterns no longer have the same power to perpetuate our confusion and reinforce our habitual tendencies. We distort reality less and less, and the very mechanisms of suffering finally disappear.

Since, at this point, we have the inner resources to deal with our emotions, our feelings of insecurity give way to freedom and confidence. We cease to be preoccupied exclusively by our hopes and fears and become available to the people around us. In this way, we bring about the welfare of others at the same time as our own.

This is a long process that develops in stages until it finally reaches fruition. All the stages of progress are beneficial. So, we should not be impatient, but persevere and appreciate the true and lasting changes that gradually occur in our way of being, rather than feeling discouraged when progress does not happen immediately.

Sources of Inspiration

Past mind has completely come to an end. Future mind has not yet occurred. Present mind is very hard to circumscribe: it has no shape, it has no colour, it is like space, insubstantial and unreal. Since this is so, one can come to realize that mind lacks intrinsic existence.

—*Atisha Dipamkara*[46]

When a rainbow appears vividly in the sky, you can see its beautiful colours, yet you could not wear it as clothing or put it on as an ornament. It arises through the conjunction of various factors, but there is nothing about it that can be grasped. Likewise, thoughts that arise in the mind have no tangible existence or intrinsic solidity. There is no logical reason why thoughts, which have no substance, should have so much power over you, nor is there any reason why you should become their slave.

The endless succession of past, present, and future thoughts leads you to believe that there is something inherently and consistently present, and you call it 'mind'. But actually... past thoughts are as dead as a corpse. Future thoughts have not yet arisen. So how could these two, which do not exist, be part of an entity that inherently exists?

However, that void nature of mind is not just a blank emptiness like empty space. There is an immediate awareness present. This clarity of mind is like the sun, illuminating the landscape and allowing you to see mountain, path, and precipice — where to go, and where not to go...

Although the mind does have this inherent awareness, to say there is 'a mind' is to give a label to something that does not exist — to assume the existence of something that is no more than a name given to a succession of events. One hundred and eight beads strung together, for example, can be called a rosary, but that 'rosary' is not a thing that exists inherently on its own. If the string breaks, where did the rosary go?

—*Dilgo Khyentse Rinpoche*[47]

Gradually I began to recognize how feeble and transitory the thoughts and emotions that had troubled me for years actually were, and how fixating on small problems had turned them into big ones. Just by sitting quietly and observing how rapidly, and in many ways illogically, my thoughts and emotions came and went, I began to recognize in a direct way that they weren't nearly as solid or real as they appeared to be. And once I began to let go of my belief in the story they seemed to tell, I began to see the 'author' beyond them — the infinitely vast, infinitely open awareness that is the nature of mind itself.

Any attempt to capture the direct experience of the

nature of mind in words is impossible. The best that can be said is that the experience is immeasurably peaceful, and, once stabilized through repeated experience, virtually unshakable. It's an experience of absolute well-being that radiates through all physical, emotional, and mental states — even those that might be ordinarily labelled as unpleasant. This sense of well-being, regardless of the fluctuation of outer and inner experiences, is one of the clearest ways to understand what Buddhists mean by 'happiness'.

—*Yongey Mingyur Rinpoche*[48]

The nature of the mind is comparable to the ocean, to the sky. The incessant movement of waves on the surface of the ocean prevents us from seeing its depths. If we dive down, there are no more waves; there is just the immense serenity of the depths... The nature of the ocean is immutable.

Look at the sky. It is sometimes clear and transparent. At other times, clouds accumulate and modify the perception we have of it. Nevertheless, the clouds do not change the nature of the sky... The mind is nothing if not a totally free nature... Remain in the natural simplicity of the mind, which is beyond all concepts.

—*Pema Wangyal Rinpoche*

Dedicating the Fruits of Our Efforts

At the end of a meditation session, before resuming your activities, it is important to make a connection between your practise and your daily life so that the good effects of the practice will last and continue to nourish inner change. If you just break off your meditation abruptly and resume your activities as though the session had never happened, it will have very little effect on your life. Its benefits will be as momentary as snowflakes falling on a hot stone.

One way of ensuring the benefits of your meditation do continue is to dedicate them through a profound aspiration whose positive energy will last until its object is realized. Here, the appropriate image is a snowflake that falls into the ocean and dissolves; it will last as long as the ocean itself.

Meditation

Arouse this aspiration: 'May the positive energy created not only by this meditation but all my good words, deeds and thoughts — past, present and future — help relieve the suffering of beings now and in the future.' Wish from the bottom of your heart for war, famine, injustice and all the suffering of poverty and physical or mental illness to be pacified through the power of what you have done.

Don't think that such a dedication of the benefits of your action is like sharing a piece of cake among a thousand people where each person receives only a few crumbs. Think that every person receives the whole piece of cake.

Also wish for all beings to find happiness, both temporary and ultimate: 'May ignorance, hatred, greed and other afflictions be eradicated from their minds, and may they completely attain all the good human qualities as well as supreme enlightenment.'

Such a dedication is an essential seal on all spiritual practice and allows the constructive energy created by your meditation and all your positive acts to be perpetuated.

Bringing Meditation and Everyday Life Together

Meditation is a process of training and transformation. For it to have meaning, it must be reflected in every aspect of your life, in all your actions and attitudes. If it is not, you have wasted your time. Therefore you have to persevere with sincerity, vigilance and determination. You need to make sure that over the course of time real changes are taking place in you. Though there is no denying that the goal of training the mind is to make us capable of maintaining a certain way of being in the midst of our activities, to say right from the beginning that your whole life and work has become a meditation is probably a bit premature. The hustle and bustle of daily life rarely provides an opening to experience the strength and stability necessary for meditative practice.

This is the reason it is important to devote time to meditation itself, even if it is only thirty minutes a day. Of course, if possible, more is better. Especially if you practise in the morning, meditation can give your day an entirely new 'fragrance'. In a subtle but profound way, its effects can permeate your outlook and approach to the things you do as well as to your relations with the people around you. As you continue through the day, you can be strengthened by the experience you have had in your formal meditation session. You will be able to refer to it inwardly because it will remain alive in your mind. During pauses in your daily activity, it will be easy for you to re-immerse yourself in the meditation experience, which is now familiar, and you will be able to maintain its beneficial effects.

Practising meditation as described above is compatible with an active professional and family life. Meditation makes it possible to see the events of your life within a larger perspective. It allows you to experience them with greater serenity without falling into indifference, to accept whatever happens without a sense of resignation and to envisage a future on the basis of altruism and confidence. Thus little by little, through training the mind, you can change your habitual way of being. You can develop a more accurate understanding of reality and a finer understanding of the laws of cause and effect, so you will be less shaken by the drastic reversals that inevitably occur in people's lives and less carried away by superficial successes. These are the signs of a genuine personal transformation, a transformation that will enable you to act more effectively in the world you live in and contribute to building a wiser and more altruistic society.

Notes

1. Romain Rolland, *Jean-Christophe*, VIII (Paris, France: Albin Michel, 1952).

2. Interview by Marc Kaufman, *Washington Post* (3 January 2005).

3. On the negative effects of stress, S. E. Sephton Ashland et al., 'Diurnal Cortisol Rhythm as a Predictor of Breast Cancer Survival', *Journal of the National Cancer Institute* 92, no. 12 (2000): 994–1000. On the influence of meditation: L. E. Carlson et al., 'Mindfulness-Based Stress Reduction in Relation to Quality of Life, Mood, Symptoms of Stress and Levels of Cortisol, Dehydroepiandrostrone-Sulftate (DHEAS) and Melatonin in Breast and Prostate Cancer Outpatients', *Psychoneuroendocrinology* 29, no. 4 (2004); M. Speca et al., 'A Randomized, Wait-List Controlled Clinical Trial: The Effect of a Mindfulness Meditation-Based Stress Reduction Program on Mood and Symptoms of Stress in Cancer Outpatients', *Psychosomatic Medicine* 62, no. 5 (September–October 2000): 613–22; S. M. Orsillo and L. Roemer (eds), *Acceptance and Mindfulness-Based Approaches to Anxiety* (Springer, 2005).

4. J. D. Teasdale et al., 'Metacognitive Awareness and Prevention of Relapse in Depression: Empirical Evidence', *Journal of Consulting and Clinical Psychology* 70 (2002): 275–87; P. Grossman et al., 'Mindfulness-Based Stress Reduction and

Health Benefits: A Meta-Analysis', *Journal of Psychosomatic Research* 57, no. 1 (2004): 35–43; S. E. Sephton et al., 'Mindfulness Meditation Alleviates Depressive Symptoms in Women with Fibromyalgia: Results of a Randomized Clinical Trial', *Arthritis Care and Research* 57, no.1 (2007): 77–85; M. A. Kenny and J. M. G. Williams, 'Treatment-Resistant Depressed Patients Show a Good Response to Mindfulness-Based Cognitive Therapy', *Behaviour Research and Therapy* 45, no. 3 (2007): 617–25.

5   MBSR – Mindfulness-Based Stress Reduction – is a non-religious form of training based on Buddhist mindfulness meditation, which was developed in the United States hospital system more than twenty years ago by Jon Kabat-Zin (see note 6 below). It is now used in more than two hundred hospitals for the palliation of post-operative pain and pain associated with cancer and other serious diseases.

6   J. Kabat-Zinn et al., 'The Clinical Use of Mindfulness Meditation for the Self-Regulation of Chronic Pain', *Journal of Behavioral Medicine* 8 (1985): 163–90.

For the long-term effects of meditation: Lutz et al., 'Long-Term Meditators,' 101, no. 46 (16 November 2004); J. A. Brefczynski-Lewis et al, 'Neural Correlates of Attentional Expertise in Long-Term Meditation Practitioners', *Proceedings of the National Academy of Sciences of the United States of America* 104, no. 27 (3 July 2007): 11483–8; P. Ekman et al., 'Buddhist and Psychological Perspectives on Emotions and Well-Being', *Current Directions in Psychological Science* 14 (2005): 59–63.

7.   A. Lutz et al., 'Attention Regulation and Monitoring in Meditation', *Trends in Cognitive Science* 12, no. 4 (April 2008): 163–9; A. P. Jha, J. Krompinger and M. J. Baime,

'Mindfulness Training Modifies Subsystems of Attention',
Cognitive Affective Behavioural Neuroscience 7 (2007): 109–19; H.
A. Slagter et al., 'Mental Training Affects Distribution of
Limited Brain Resources', *PLoS Biology* 5, no. 6 (June 2007):
138.

8.   L. E. Carlson et al., 'One Year Pre-Post Intervention
     Follow-Up of Psychological, Immune, Endocrine and Blood
     Pressure Outcomes of Mindfulness-Based Stress Reduction
     (MBSR) in Breast and Prostate Cancer Out Patients', *Brain
     Behavior and Immunity* 21 (2007): 1038–49.

9.   See P. Grossman, 'Mindfulness-Based Stress Reduction'.

10. A. Lutz, J. D. Dunne and R. J. Davidson, 'Meditation and
     the Neuroscience of Consciousness: An Introduction', in
     The Cambridge Handbook of Consciousness, eds P. D. Zelazo, M.
     Moscovitch and E. Thompson (Cambridge, Cabridge
     University Press, 2008), 497–549.

11. Yongey Mingyur Rinpoche, *The Joy of Living*, 32.

12. Jigme Khyentse Rinpoche, oral teachings, Portugal,
     September 2007.

13. A Buddhist author of the seventh century, whose principal
     work, *Entering the Way of the Bodhisattva*, is a great classic.

14. Dalai Lama, *Ancient Wisdom, Modern World, Ethics for the Next
     Millenium* (London: Abacus, 2001).

15. Attributed to Nagarjuna.

16. Nagarjuna, *Nagarjuna's Letter to a Friend (Suhrllekha)*, with
     commentary by Kyabje Kangyur Rinpoche, trans.
     Padmakara Translation Group (Ithaca, NY: Snow Lion
     Publications, 2006), 49.

17. Shantideva, *The Way of the Bodhisattva*, trans. Padmakara Translation Group (Boston: Shambhala Publications, 2003), 37.

18. Dilgo Khyentse Rinpoche (1910–91) was one of the most eminent Tibetan spiritual masters of the twentieth century. This quote is from *The Heart Treasure of the Enlightened Ones*, 51–2.

19. Bhante Henepola Gunaratna, *Mindfulness in Plain English*, 134.

20. Thich Nhat Hanh, *Guide de la méditation marchée* (Village des Pruniers,France: Editions La Bôi, 1983).

21. In Sanskrit, these three elements are called *manaskara*, *smriti* and *samprajnana*. The equivalent Pali terms are *manasikara*, *sati* and *sampajanna*. The Tibetan terms are *yid la byed pa*, *dran pa* and *shes bzhin*.

22. A mantra is not generally constructed like a phrase with a literal meaning. Here 'om' is the syllable that opens the mantra and confers on it a power of transformation. 'Mani', or jewel, refers to the jewel of altruistic love and compassion. 'Padme', the genitive form of *padma* or lotus, refers to the fundamental nature of consciousness, our 'original goodness', which, as a lotus rises immaculately out of the mud, remains intact even in the midst of the mental poisons we have fabricated. 'Hum' is the syllable that gives the mantra its power of accomplishment.

23. Padmasambhava, *Natural Liberation: Padmasambhava's Teachings on the Six Bardos*, trans. and ed. B. Alan Wallace (Boston: Wisdom Publications, 1998), 113.

24. Shabkar, *The Life of Shabkar, The Autobiography of a Tibetan Yogin*, (Ithaca, NY: Snow Lion Publications, 2001), 535.

25. Bokar Rinpoche, *La méditation, conseils aux débutants* (Sainte-Cannat, France: Editions Claire Lumière, 1999), 73.

26. Yongey Mingyur Rinpoche, *The Joy of Living*, 178.

27. Shantideva, *The Way of the Bodhisattva*, 51–2.

28. Shantideva, Ibid., 169.

29. 'Pain', in the series entitled *Documentary*, directed by Andrew North, BBC World Service, February 2008.

30. Yongey Mingyur Rinpoche, *The Joy of Living*, 147.

31. Bhante Henepola Gunaratna, *Mindfulness in Plain English*, 131–2.

32. Longchen Rabjam, *gsung thor bu* (Paro, Bhutan: Lama Ngodrub and Sherab Drimey, 1982).

33. Extracted from *mkha' gdams kyi skyes bu dam pa rnams kyi gsung bgros thor bu ba rnams*, translated by Matthieu Ricard, 89.

34. The eight worldly preoccupations are gain and loss, pleasure and pain, praise and blame, fame and obscurity.

35. Dilgo Khyentse Rinpoche, *The Hundred Verses of Advice: Tibetan Buddhist Teachings on What Matters Most*, trans. Padmakara Translation Group (Boston: Shambhala Publications, 2006), 131.

36. Teachings given in Schneeverdingen, Germany, in 1998. Oral translation by Matthieu Ricard.

37. Thich Nhat Hanh, *The Sun in my Heart* (Berkley, CA: Parallax Press, 1988), 8.

38. Bhante Henepola Gunaratna, *Mindfulness in Plain English*, 127.

39. Nagarjuna, *Nagarjuna's Letter to a Friend*, 98.

40. Etty Hillesum, *An Interrupted Life* (New York: Holt Paperbacks, 1996), 212.

41. Ibid., 84.

42. Dalai Lama, *Conseils du Coeur* (Paris, Presses de la Renaissance), 130–1.

43. Dilgo Khyentse Rinpoche, *The Heart Treasure of the Enlightened Ones*.

44. Ibid., 92

45. Han F. de Wit, *The Spiritual Path: An Introduction to the Psychology of the Spiritual Traditions* (Pitttsburgh, PA: Duquesne University Press, 1999).

46. Atisha Dipamkara, *Essential Instructions on the Middle Way*, translated by Matthieu Ricard.

47. Dilgo Khyentse Rinpoche, *The Heart of Compassion*, 141–2.

48. Yongey M. Rinpoche, *The Joy of Living*, 21–2.

Bibliography

Bhante Henepola Gunaratna, *Mindfulness in Plain English*, Somerville, MA: Wisdom Publications, 2002

Bokar Rinpoche, *La méditation, conseils aux débutants*, Sainte-Cannat, France: Editions Claire Lumière, 1999

Bokar Rinpoche, *Meditation: Advice to Beginners*, San Fransisco: Clearpoint Press, 1993

Buddhdasa Bhikkhu, *Mindfulness with Breathing*, Somerville, MA:Wisdom Publications, 1988

Dalai Lama, *A Flash of Lightning in the Dark of Night: A Guide to the Bodhisattva's Way of Life*, Boston: Shambhala Publications, 1994

Dilgo Khyentse Rinpoche, *The Hundred Verses of Advice: Tibetan Buddhist Teachings on What Matters Most*, Boston: Shambhala Publications, 2006

———, *The Heart Treasure of the Enlightened Ones: The Practice of View, Meditation, and Action*, Boston: Shambhala Publications, 1993

———, *The Heart of Compassion: The Thirty-seven Verses on the Practice of a Bodhisattva*, Boston: Shambhala Publications, 2007

Dudjom Rinpoche, *Counsels from my Heart*, Boston: Shambhala Publications, 2003

Dzigar Kongtrul, *It's Up to You: The Practice of Self-Reflection on the Buddhist Path*, Boston: Shambhala Publications, 2006

Kunzang Pelden, *The Nectar of Manjushri's Speech, a Detailed Commentary on Shantideva's Way of the Bodhisattva*, Boston, Shambhala Publications, 2007

Longchen Yeshe Dorje (Kangyur Rinpoche), trans. Padmakara Translation Group, *The Treasury of Precious Qualities: A Commentary on the Root Text of Jigme Lingpa*, Boston: Shambhala Publications, 2001, revised 2009

Patrul Rinpoche, *The Words of My Perfect Teacher*, Boston: Shambhala Publications, 1998

Ricard, Matthieu, *Happiness: A Guide to Developing Life's Most Important Skill*, Boston: Little Brown, 2006; London: Atlantic Books, 2007

Ringu Tulku, *Path to Buddhahood*, Boston: Shambhala Publications, 2003

Shabkar, *The Life of Shabkar, The Autobiography of a Tibetan Yogin*, Ithaca, NY: Snow Lion Publications, 2001

Shantideva, *The Way of the Bodhisattva: (Bodhicaryavatara)*, Boston: Shambhala Publications, 1997

Tulku Pema Wangyal, *L'esprit d'éveil, Bodhicitta*, Saint-Léon-sur-Vézère, France: Editions Padmakara, 1997

Thich Nhat Hanh, *Miracle of Mindfulness*, Boston: Beacon Press, 1999

Yongey Mingyur Rinpoche and Swanson, Eric, *The Joy of Living*, New York: Three Rivers Press, 2008

Wallace, B. Alan, *Choosing Reality*, Ithica, NY: Snow Lion Publications, 2003

———, *The Attention Revolution, Unlocking the Power of the Focused Mind*, Somerville, MA: Wisdom Publications, 2006

Acknowledgements

I would like to thank all those who made this book possible.

Needless to say, I owe everything of worth in it to the goodness and wisdom of my spiritual masters, the main ones being Kyabje Kangyur Rinpoche, Dilgo Khyentse Rinpoche, Trulshik Rinpoche, Pema Wangyal Rinpoche and Jigme Khyentse Rinpoche, as well as His Holiness the Dalai Lama, who, according to the great teachers I have just mentioned, is the most accomplished Tibetan Buddhist master of our time.

I would also like to thank all those who urged me to gather together these instructions on meditation because they wanted to meditate. Without them, the idea of composing this small work would not have entered my mind.

I would like to thank my loyal publisher Nicole Lattés, who has always encouraged me to continue with my efforts despite my lack of natural literary talent.

I am also very grateful to those friends who have had the patience to read this text and who have improved it considerably both in form and substance through their informed suggestions: Christian Bruyat, Carisse and Gérard Busquet, my dear mother, Yahne Le Toumelin, Raphaële Demandre, Gérard Godet, Christophe André and Michel Bitbol.

My deep gratitude goes to Sherab Chödzin Kohn, who patiently and skilfully translated this book into English, to Vivian Kurz for helping to significantly improve the text, to my editors, Patty Gift and Sarah Norman, and to my publishers Atlantic Books and Hay House.

The author's royalties from this book will be entirely dedicated to humanitarian projects in Tibet, Nepal and India, and to the preservation of the Himalayan cultural heritage. Anyone wishing to join in this effort, may contact www.karuna-shechen.org and www.shechen.org.